FANTASTIC BEASTS
AND WHERE TO FIND THEM

MOVIE-MAKING NEWS
THE STORIES BEHIND THE MAGIC

EXCLUSIVE INTERVIEWS ✦ FILMMAKING FACTS ✦ PREVIOUSLY UNTOLD TALES

JODY REVENSON

Discover all the behind-the-scenes secrets
from the first film and get a sneak peek at...

FANTASTIC BEASTS
THE CRIMES OF GRINDELWALD

WIZARDING WORLD

HARPER DESIGN
An Imprint of HarperCollins Publishers

FIRST PUBLISHED BY HARPER DESIGN

195 BROADWAY, NEW YORK, NEW YORK 10007.

TEL: (212) 207-7000 FAX: (855) 746-6023

HARPERDESIGN@HARPERCOLLINS.COM

WWW.HC.COM

Text by Jody Revenson

HarperCollins books may be purchased for educational, business, or sales promotional use.
For information please e-mail the Special Markets Department at SPsales@harpercollins.com.

PROJECT EDITOR:	PAGE LAYOUT:	COVER DESIGN:	PRODUCTION MANAGER:
Chris Smith	Terence Caven	Holly Macdonald	Simon Moore

HARPERCOLLINS WOULD LIKE TO THANK

**VICTORIA SELOVER, EMMA WHITTARD, MICKEY STERN,
JILL BENSCOTER, MELANIE SWARTZ, KATIE MACKAY,
KATIE KHAN, NATALIE LAVERICK & ROSS FRASER**

ISBN 978-0-06-285308-0

PRINTED AND BOUND BY RR DONNELLEY APS, CHINA
FIRST PRINTING, 2018

CONTENTS

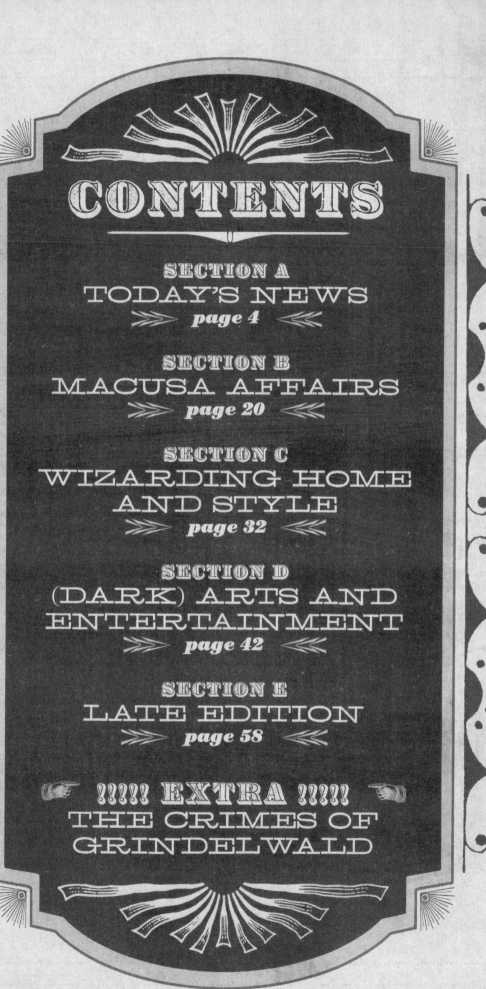

!!!!! EXTRA !!!!!
THE CRIMES OF GRINDELWALD

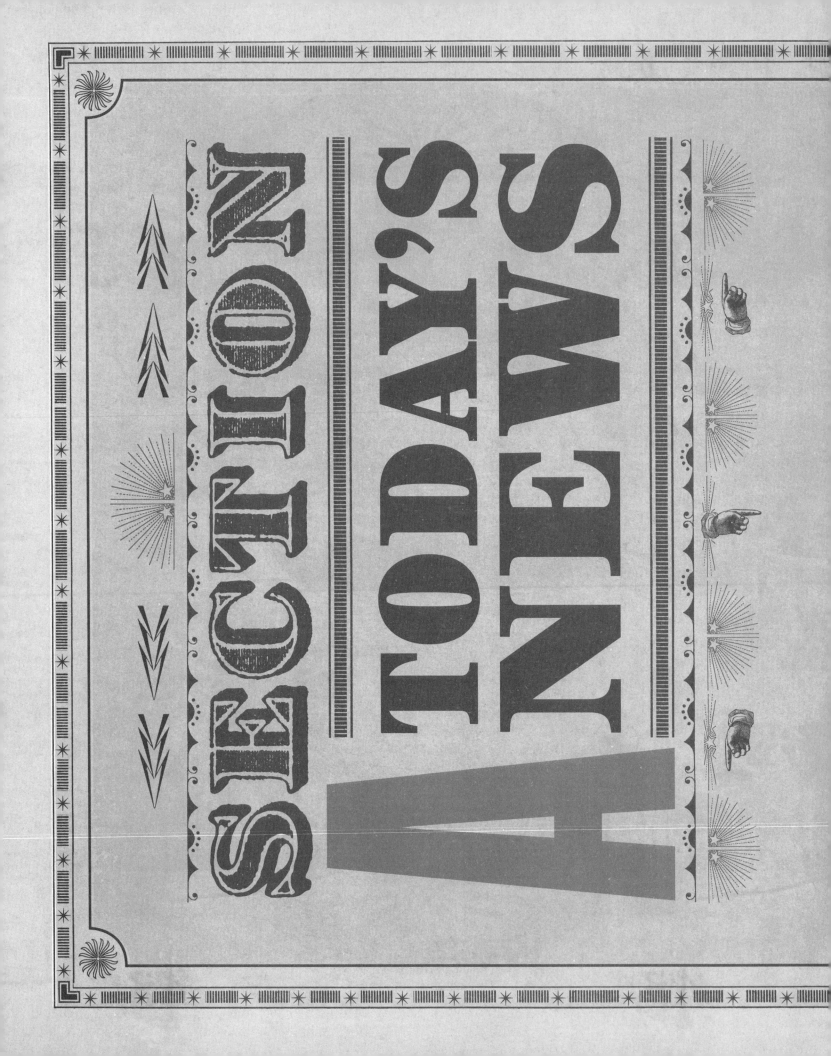

SECTION A

TODAY'S NEWS

DARK WIZARD, DARKENING TIMES

GRINDELWALD
WANTS TO EXPOSE THE MAGICAL WORLD

FOR MORE NEWS SEE PAGE 72

AS *FANTASTIC BEASTS AND WHERE TO FIND THEM* BEGINS, THE DARK WIZARD GELLERT GRINDELWALD HAS STAGED A SERIES OF ATTACKS ON THE MUGGLE COMMUNITY IN EUROPE, AND AMERICAN WIZARDS ARE BECOMING FEARFUL THAT GRINDELWALD'S CAMPAIGN WILL COME TO THE UNITED STATES.

The wizarding world in America has already endured a deadly intolerance of their community in the 1692 witch trials of Salem, Massachusetts. Since then, wizarding laws were developed stating that there should be little or no interaction between magical and non-magical populations, to ensure the safety of wizards. These laws enforce a total segregation between the wizarding and No-Maj communities, including marriage.

WORLD ORDER THREATENED

'So witches and wizards in New York in 1926 are very discreet' says *Fantastic Beasts and Where to Find Them* director David Yates. 'They're a hidden community. If you walked down Fifth Avenue, you'd probably pass one without realizing it. Ultimately they come up against a force that threatens to expose them, and that becomes a fulcrum point in our story.'

'What Grindelwald wants to do is expose the magical world,' producer David Heyman explains, 'and in so doing, create a war with the non-wizarding world. And there is the fear that a fascist, someone who is intolerant as Grindelwald is, will cause nothing but pain.'

While Grindelwald appears only briefly in the movie, the underlying theme of a disenfranchised society and the machinations used by policymakers to take advantage of that weaves into the narrative. 'These are themes of Jo's that have interested her forever,' says Heyman. 'I don't think we set out to make a political film with a capital P. This is an entertainment with themes that resonate across time. Alas, some of the issues we face in this film are timeless.'

The name 'Gellert Grindelwald' strikes fear among the wizarding community as seen in a series of newspaper articles that help set the stage for the story of *Fantastic Beasts and Where to Find Them*.

Gellert Grindelwald is recruiting an army of supporters who follow his warped ideas about the superiority of wizards over No-Majs, and who, if not stopped, could help him seize power over the entire wizarding community.

After wreaking havoc on the continent, this powerful Dark wizard has slipped away, and is nowhere to be found. If he is not stopped, Grindelwald's attacks could incite a war with the No-Majs. His attacks are increasing, so the population has been warned to be on alert.

BREAKING NEWS SEE PAGE 77

GRINDELWALD'S GOALS

IS GRINDELWALD RIGHT?

'There are those people who believe it's pathetic, I suppose, that wizards are still living in hiding,' adds Eddie Redmayne, who plays Newt Scamander. 'That there should be a vocal war against Muggles. I suppose there's a certain peace at the moment, but Grindelwald is stirring that up. He believes in the superiority of the wizarding community over the Muggle community.'

UNEXPLAINED ACTIVITY IN MANHATTAN

MACUSA officials suspect a magical force has been causing destruction in the city and drawing the attention of No-Majs. Without warning, streets shake and then explode like earthquakes, their cobblestones hurling into the air, causing damage to cars and nearby buildings, which are left in rubble. Cars are raised up and blown across the street; manhole covers have similarly blasted out of their frames. This activity is often accompanied by a roar or a howl.

A witness to one event described it: 'It was like a — like a *wind* or a — like a *ghost* — but dark — and I saw its eyes — shinin' white eyes — like a dark mass, and it dove down there, down underground — I swear to God . . . into the earth right in front of me.'

While it was initially thought the force was located in an isolated area, it has wreaked havoc in several neighbourhoods, though most notably the Lower East Side and in the City Hall area.

SECOND SALEMERS AND THEIR CAMPAIGN TO EXPOSE AND WIPE OUT WIZARDING KIND

Led by the extremist Mary Lou Barebone, the NSPS, also known as the 'Second Salemers,' hearkens back to the original Salem Witch Trials, which took place in the late 1600s in Massachusetts.

'Mary Lou Barebone is this evangelical-type character with a strong belief that witches exist in New York, and she wants to out them,' explains David Yates. 'She wants to bring to the attention of every regular New Yorker that these witches exist in New York. The Barebones represent this very eerie, strange fringe of the story that is actually the story.'

Ezra Miller, who plays Credence Barebone, Mary Lou's oldest adopted child, describes the Second Salemers as 'caught up in a modality that is evil. When I read the script it felt like a culmination of so many of the ideas that had been subtly present in the works that precede this. [J.K. Rowling] takes very big ideas, and reduces them down to a quintessential form in a specific story. I think she's truly a master of that.'

'Mary Lou is a very important character because she's onto the wizards,' says Rowling. 'On the surface, [she's] quite a kind woman. She's feeding poor children in the street. But in fact she's intensely abusive.'

EVIL, AYE

'**I** think there'll be a place carved out for the ominous vibes of Mary Lou Barebone,' says Ezra Miller. 'Samantha delivered an unbelievably, yes, evil, but also unbelievably complex and morally ambiguous and realistically grounded performance.'

OCEAN CROSSINGS

BEHIND THE BAREBONES

Mary Lou Barebone, played by Samantha Morton, does, indeed, seem quite a kind woman, who feeds homeless and destitute children in exchange for their help in distributing her propaganda against the magical community. She's adopted three children: Credence, Chastity, and Modesty. 'They're not related to each other,' says Jenn Murray, who plays Chastity, 'and they've all come together to live under this roof in a church. They're not well off. They believe very strongly in their faith, and that "if you don't follow our way, you're wrong, and bad things will happen to you."' Murray makes an understatement when she describes the family as having a 'complicated relationship. They're all very connected to each other, yet they're all very isolated.'

'There is darkness to this film,' says Eddie Redmayne. 'There's brutality to it. The themes of repression and segregation and what happens when you are forced to oppress things . . . I found really moving.'

> ## SEE RELATED COVERAGE
> ### ➤ IN SECTION D ➡
> #### SECOND SALEMERS' SIGN SIGNALS STRONG STATEMENT

PORT OF NEW YORK ARRIVAL FOR THESEUS SCAMANDER'S BROTHER

New to New York's shores is Newt Scamander, a self-proclaimed 'Magizoologist' who is currently researching a book about fantastic beasts. Scamander hails from England, where there are much softer restrictions about magical creatures. So who is Newt Scamander? Born to a respected wizarding family, Newton Artemis Fido Scamander attended Hogwarts School of Witchcraft and Wizardry (Hufflepuff house) but was expelled before graduation. During the Great War, he worked with Ukrainian Ironbellies on the Eastern Front. His older brother, Theseus, is a war hero, and Head of the Auror Office at the British Ministry of Magic. The younger Scamander has recently spent a year in the field for his work.

The character of Newt Scamander began life as the author of a book called *Fantastic Beasts and Where To Find Them*, written by author J.K. Rowling to raise money for Comic Relief in 2001. 'During the writing of that textbook, I became quite interested in the ostensible author,

CONTINUED ON PAGE 11

IS ROGUE AUTHOR'S 'RESEARCH' A THREAT?

'HE SIMPLY WANTS TO GET HIS CREATURES BACK IN HIS CASE AND GET OUT OF THERE,' SAYS DAVID YATES.

As the story begins, 'Newt's been travelling the world studying magical creatures,' Rowling explains. 'His ambition is write *Fantastic Beasts and Where to Find Them*. He wants people to understand how remarkable these creatures are, and he wants to educate the public to stop them killing them. But Newt being Newt, if he finds something that's injured or endangered, he can't resist taking it with him.'

'Newt's the only person who has that job in the entire wizarding world,' says director David Yates, 'because nobody really thinks beasts are a good idea to get involved with: they're dangerous, and some can kill you!'

Despite the danger, Newt is much more comfortable with the creatures than he is with human beings. 'He's slightly awkward in his own skin,' Rowling continues. 'In the animal world, though, he's completely at home.'

Rowling explains that Newt comes from a Ministry family who are very much about getting the promotion, upholding the law. 'But Newt doesn't like authority,' says Eddie Redmayne. 'He didn't love the Ministry when he was working there. He's his own boss, and he always has been. He sees the wonder and the brilliance in these animals and he believes that the wizarding community, with a proper education, could learn to live side by side with these animals and appreciate how extraordinary they are.

'What I love about Newt is he's a passionate fellow,' Redmayne continues. 'He's got his own interests and lives his own life. He's got his own agenda. He's not a people-pleaser.' (In fact, at one point Newt knowingly tells Jacob, 'I annoy people.') 'He's very content in his own company and in the company of his animals. It's only throughout the film you realize that for all the wonder and excitement of his life, there is a hole there in some ways. There is a part of him where there's a sadness. One of the wonderful journeys for him in the film is about human contact. He's learning to be himself, really.'

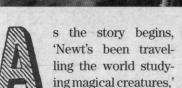

CONFRONTING THE UNKNOWN

During Newt's journey, he's exposed to the prejudice and secrecy that pervades the North American wizarding community. 'He's walked into a situation he doesn't understand at all,' says Rowling. 'Something that has implications for the whole wizarding world. He doesn't really understand how the magic works here and he accidentally opens a case of magical creatures in the middle of New York in arguably the most hostile place he could have done this,' she continues. 'He's blundered hugely and all of that is massive fun to write.'

> 'THERE IS A PART OF HIM WHERE THERE'S A SADNES'
> **— EDDIE REDMAYNE**

CONTINUED FROM PAGE 9

Newt Scamander,' says Rowling, 'and of all the characters in Potter who were just a name, he was the one who took on quite a bit of life in my mind.' When Warner Bros. came to J.K. Rowling with the idea of developing the book into a film, she started collecting her thoughts on Newt's backstory and, twelve days later, had written a very rough screenplay.

A MAGIZO-OLOGIST'S MOVEMENT

Eddie Redmayne did quite a lot of research for his part, meeting with zoologists and safari park personnel. 'They all talked passionately about their techniques and their methods,' he remembers. 'I met with people who dealt with the breeding of animals, and heard stories that, for example, when new cubs were born, the guys or girls would literally sleep in their beds with them.'

Redmayne also worked with people whose trade is to track animals for a living. 'Seeing how these trackers walked brought physical elements to Newt's way of walking. For example, when they're trying to pursue an animal they have to be incredibly silent. They turn their feet and legs out, and they'll lift one leg and place it exactly where they want it, with deliberation. And there's a kind of open stance that I adopted.' Research also included working with the descriptions J.K. Rowling had written in her script. 'She wrote that when you see Newt walking down the New York streets for the first time, he has an "unselfconscious [Buster] Keatonesque" quality, a "sense of different rhythm to those around him." I desperately tried to work out what that was!'

TRIED AND TRUSTED

The bank's first floor interior was filmed at Martins Bank in Liverpool, with tall marble columns in cream, and red, and brown, and gold-gated tellers' windows. Production designer Stuart Craig looked for the same principles he applied to using Australia House in London for Gringotts Bank to choose the location for the bank. 'Banks, then more than now, were out to impress you with their magnificence and inspire confidence.' Martins has all that and more.

'When you first meet Jacob [Kowalski], he's back from the war,' says Dan Fogler, who plays the promising baker. 'He's like the *last guy* back from the war, like no one told him it was over. So now he's looking to start a family and open a bakery.' Jacob brings a suitcase full of his pastries to show to the loan manager, Mr Bingley (Peter Breitmayer). 'He knows that if [Bingley] just tastes one of these pastries, he's going to get the loan.' Newt, in the meantime, has followed the Niffler into the bank and meets up with Jacob as he waits for his appointment. Newt bears an identical case — except his case is full of magical creatures.

Jacob doesn't get the loan, but he has picked up an Occamy egg Newt left on the bench, and the egg is starting to hatch. The Niffler, meanwhile, has been scurrying through the bank, causing mayhem in its hunt for anything glittery — Nifflers will snatch or steal whatever shiny object catches their eye and store it in the pouch on their belly, which can hold a considerable amount. Newt is torn between getting the egg and getting the Niffler, and makes the choice to magically summon Jacob and Disapparate to a lower level staircase. 'This,' says director David Yates, 'is the moment where we reveal that Newt Scamander, this man who has arrived in New York in 1926, is, in fact, a wizard.'

Newt takes Jacob along for the ride in his efforts to recapture his creature when

COMMOTION
AT NO-MAJ BANK

CONTINUED ON PAGE 14

ANIMATING BEASTS

TO CREATE BELIEVABLE BEASTS, MAGIC IS ALWAYS GROUNDED IN REALISM

For the Harry Potter films, creatures were conceived by development artists, and then their images were converted into three-dimensional maquettes, with complete colouring and textures. The maquettes were cyberscanned for the visual effects artists to bring to life with movement and expression. *Fantastic Beasts and Where to Find Them* bypassed much of this process by going directly from two-dimensional concepts to three-dimensional digital versions. To that end, the visual artists were brought on at the film's outset. 'We were given a lot of creative freedom from the beginning,' says Pablo Grillo, the senior animation supervisor for Framestore. Grillo was in charge of the movement, performance, action and design of many of the characters. 'David [Yates] saw the value in bringing the animation team in from the start, to shape how these creatures were going to come together.

There was almost an alarming level of trust in us and the team,' he says with a laugh. 'We were put in charge of overseeing how the animals were going to grow into real characters, and not just the flat images we drew them as.' For several months, the animators created creature situations and funny moments with Yates and the producers before selecting the group that made it into the final film. 'From there we could start to formulate

> 'DAVID SAW THE VALUE IN BRINGING THE ANIMATION TEAM IN FROM THE START TO SHAPE HOW THESE CREATURES WERE GOING TO COME TOGETHER'
> – PABLO GRILLO

behaviour and visual gags; little quirks that actually informed the final script, and build them into the big set pieces. It was an incredibly fulfilling process overall, mainly because of the challenges open to us.'

REAL-LIFE RESOURCES

For inspiration, photographic references were gathered of real-world possibilities, including moles, platypuses, and echidnas. 'And we gathered video resources of animals using their hands,' says Grillo. 'Platypuses were very charming, constantly churning and looking through the silt and sand for food.' Another video reference was of a honey badger. 'We found great footage of a honey badger in South Africa ransacking somebody's house,' says visual effects supervisor Christian Manz. 'It was just an insatiable desire for food, going through fridges and cupboards. A lot of those real-world animalistic traits are what went into the Niffler. Which is why I think he's so successful, because he's all of those things.'

Grillo also asked the animators to look at YouTube compilations of animal 'fails.' 'One, they're very funny,' he admits. 'But they're also a brilliant insight into animal psychology, which is different from humans. More often than not these animals want to jump across a gap or across a space and they screw it up or miscalculate it. It's a conflict between their desire and what their body is able to pull off in the end. I think that's what brings the charm — the clumsiness of that physicality juxtaposed against the desire.'

GRAPHIC DESIGN OF ADVERT BY MINA LIMA

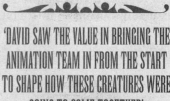

NABBING A NIFFLER

'Who is the Niffler?' ponders Eddie Redmayne. 'The Niffler is the bane of my life. He's one of my favourite beasts but he causes carnage.' Following the Niffler, Newt and Jacob find themselves inside the bank's vault, then almost arrested for robbery, not what Newt, or Jacob, needed. 'It all goes horribly, horribly wrong, and this one catalyst sets in motion an insane amount of events that just cause all kinds of chaos,' says Redmayne. 'The Niffler has such character that Newt can't help but love him despite the fact that he is endlessly causing him trouble. I've got to say he is a bit of a favourite.'

The bank sequence is 'driven by the relationship between Newt and the Niffler,' explains Framestore animator Andras Ormos. 'There was a history we had to get across, the fact that the Niffler was notorious for escaping and pickpocketing, and that Newt was going through the motions in trying to catch him. They understood each other; there were little looks, a language in their movement.'

'And how is it going to get around that space undetected?' Pablo Grillo adds. 'How's it going to get away from Newt? You become the Niffler to a degree.' In fact, he *literally* became the Niffler at times. Throughout filming, Grillo,

MURTLAP ATTACKS NO-MAJ

When Jacob Kowalski returns to his apartment at 435 Rivington Street, he discovers the case he has brought home is not his when the latches release themselves and he hears strange growling noises. Then the lid opens up and he is attacked by an angry Murtlap.

Symptoms of a Murtlap bite for witches or wizards include an itchy rash and a minor resistance to curses and jinxes. No-Majes who are bitten experience profuse sweating, with a more serious reaction indicated by flames out of their anus.

The Murtlap is described as a rat-like creature with an anemone-style growth on its back, which made the concept artists' job very easy. 'I suppose there's not a lot of possibilities for a rat-like creature with a sea anemone on its back,' quips concept artist Dermot Power. Visual artist Paul Catling needed only one pass at drawing it to nail the design.

in addition to many puppeteers, often worked with a representation of a creature while scenes were staged. During rehearsals, these puppets would provide proper eye lines, but also interact with the actors in order for them to understand the size, shape, movement, and most importantly, the character of the creature. While in the bank vault, Newt has to relieve the Niffler of all the sparkling, glittering objects he's collected. During his research for the part, Redmayne spent time with a zoologist who was working with a baby anteater. 'It would curl up into a little ball, and in order to make it relax, she would tickle his little belly,' he says. 'There's a moment where the Niffler has gorged himself on glittery stuff, and Newt is trying to get him to release his jewels. So he ends up tickling him.'

CONTINUED FROM PAGE **12**

he spots the Niffler squeezing into the bank's vault. 'I was really inspired by lots of Buster Keaton, Charlie Chaplin movies of the 1920s,' says Yates, who describes the Niffler as 'a cheeky, beautiful, odd, greedy, kind of ferrety little guy who adores shiny things and has got a very tricky relationship with Newt. Newt's always chasing him everywhere, and the Niffler's always trying to get away.'

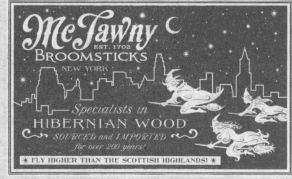

THE CASE OF SWITCHED CASES

UNKNOWN TO JACOB KOWALSKI AND NEWT SCAMANDER, THEY ACCIDENTALLY SWITCHED CASES OUTSIDE THE BANK AS JACOB MADE HIS ESCAPE FROM THE CONFUSING SITUATION.

Jacob returns to his apartment, overwhelmed by everything that happened that morning. 'Then I open what I think is my case and out pour all these creatures,' says Fogler. 'One after another in my apartment, breaking down the walls, and when the Murtlap comes out he bites me.'

Newt and Tina Goldstein, a witch who was trailing Newt at the bank, are trying to track down Jacob to Obliviate him, and come upon the destruction caused by the creatures who have escaped Newt's case. 'So Newt finds me,' Fogler continues. 'He realizes, "Not only do I have to get all these creatures back, now I have to look after this No-Maj, because he might die, because he's been bitten by this thing." So I get pulled along on the adventure with them trying to collect all the creatures and get safely back home.'

Jacob Kowalski is the first major character in any wizarding story by J.K. Rowling who is non-magical. 'Can you imagine walking into the wizarding world as someone who's never even witnessed or experienced magic before?' says producer David Heyman. 'That sense of wonder, that sense of how extraordinary it is, is felt and seen through Jacob.'

'Jacob is the innocent in this world,' says Rowling. 'He accidentally tangles with this wizard [Newt], and then he's along for this crazy ride that he shouldn't be on.'

'One of the more delightful aspects of the story is that ultimately you're taken into it with Jacob, who drops into this sort of extraordinary world,' says director David Yates. 'and we *are* Jacob. We experience many of these things from his point of view, and that's a very good point actually.' Yates remembers that Jacob was a difficult part to cast until Fogler walked in. 'Dan was the only guy who read the part of Jacob and surprised us with it. We had loads of actors who would do a really straight version of Jacob, and then Dan came and inverted it. He did things that were sad when they should've been funny, and funny when they should have been sad. That gift and quality made us go "Wow, he's gonna steal this."'

Actor Dan Fogler had no doubt that he could relate to his character. 'I am Jacob, you know. I *am* Jacob entering this very magical wizarding world. I was like a kid in a candy store.'

AUTHENTIC DELICIOUSNESS

Dan Fogler has another reason for thinking it was kismet that he played the part of a baker for the film. 'I knew all the names of the streets that we were running down, and I knew the character really well, because my grandfather was a baker,' Fogler explains. 'He had the best pumpernickel in New York; that's what he was known for.' Fogler believes his family legacy is a contributing reason to his winning the part. 'Because they saw my tape and said, "Oh, this guy knows this character." Because he's very much in my blood.'

PERHAPS NO-MAJ CLARION IS 'NEWS YOU CAN TRUST'?

SECOND SALEMERS IGNORED BY CLARION NEWSPAPER

The *New York Clarion*, local No-Maj newspaper, owned and operated by Henry Shaw Sr, father of New York Senator Henry Shaw Jr, denies the legitimacy of the New Salem Philanthropic Society despite the protests of Shaw's younger son, Langdon.

Langdon Shaw, played by Ronan Raftery, is convinced he's uncovered something very strange going on in the city. 'He's trying to spread the word that it's witches and wizards causing the disturbances,' explains Raftery. 'He wants people to understand why all these strange things in the city are happening, but nobody will listen, so I'm a very, very frustrated figure through most of my scenes!' Raftery made up a backstory for himself about Langdon, not seen in the movie, that he's been talking to the New Salem Philanthropic Society. 'And he believes everything they have to say. So I bring them to my father, an incredibly powerful newspaper magnate, to blow this story open, to get him to print this, to get him

to tell the world what's going on in the city.'

Langdon's father, Henry Shaw Sr, is played by veteran actor Jon Voight. Henry Sr does not listen to his younger son — he's more concerned with Henry Jr getting re-elected to the senate. Josh Cowdery plays the older brother who does not see eye-to-eye with his sibling. As far as Henry Jr is concerned, 'I'm the chosen golden child,' says Cowdery. 'Ronan plays the younger brother who makes all the mistakes and gets involved in all the wrong stuff. He wants to prove himself by bringing in this anti-witch group who are trying to use the newspaper's power for themselves. It's a pretty stressful time for us,' Cowdery continues, 'and then Langdon brings in the Barebone family. We're on opposing sides as far as the grounded, non-magical world and the belief in magic. You can immediately see these two groups are not friends.' Henry Jr unknowingly makes a bigger mistake than his brother when he disdainfully tells the Barebones to leave, and calls Credence a 'freak.'

SECOND SALEMER SON UNDER HIS MOTHER'S WING

Credence Barebone is 'an outsider who's misunderstood,' says David Yates, 'trying to find his place in the world, who has very special skills and very special things going on.' In that way Credence sounds a bit like Harry Potter, but he couldn't be more the opposite. Colin Farrell, whose character, Auror Percival Graves, has an intriguing relationship with Credence, describes him as 'a young man who, like many young men, seems lost in his life, like the world is a mystery to him, as he is a mystery to himself also. Graves is taking the lead and there's a little bit of guidance, a little bit of support and tenderness, and there's a little bit of manipulation.'

Credence is regularly abused by his mother, who whips him with a belt, and reminds him that his real mother was a

wicked, unnatural woman. 'We all see ourselves struggle with trauma,' says Ezra Miller, 'and see people that struggle in more acute and severe ways. It was important for me to explore the tough choice of how that trauma is gonna manifest in the rest of their life. Whether that wound will be a blessing or it will be a curse.'

'I think it's rare that something can come from a world of fantasy and really touch upon something that painful and that delicate. And for me, the opportunity to flesh that out from both the magical and the human perspective is an amazing gift.' Miller continues, 'I think you can't run from who you are. Well, you can, but when it does catch up to you, there are going to be heavy consequences.'

For Credence, 'I really wanted him to almost be like somebody who was pulling in,' says Colleen Atwood. She took what she called a 'meanness' to his costumes, giving him a high, tight collar; tightness in the shoulders, and a slight bug-shape outline to his jacket. Tight striped pants were added and gave him 'a weird marionette shape.' Credence and Jacob are the only two characters in the movie who don't have a coat, which Atwood did on purpose. 'There's a poverty to not having a coat in the coldness, and I really liked that for Credence.'

OUT OF FASHION

Beneath Credence's pork-pie style hat is an unusual haircut. 'I found a picture in a French portrait book,' Atwood recalls. 'It's almost like somebody shaved the back of your head with a bowl on the front but with a fringe. I showed it to David [Yates] and said, "I know it's out there, but I would love for Credence to have that haircut."' Yates loved it.

Under Credence's full costume is one other item. 'Because I'm sure you're all wondering, I'm wearing 1920s underwear under the costume,' says Ezra Miller. 'Just for me, so that I know it's that real. I just wanted to share that,' he says with a laugh.

A SIMPLE PALOOKA

THE RELATIONSHIP BETWEEN JACOB AND NEWT CHANGES AS THE STORY PROGRESSES.

Early on, Fogler thought of Jacob as Newt's Sherpa. 'I'm his guide in the city, because he doesn't know New York very well.' Fogler then grew to think of them as like Sherlock and Watson or Don Quixote and Sancho Panza. 'A classic, iconic pairing,' as he describes it. 'It's pulling from these classic, iconic archetypes. Newt is a fish out of water. He's very cerebral and Charles Darwin-like with his creatures, and Jacob's the blue-collar guy who knows the streets. So we balance each other out in that regard.

'And then we find out he's not such a regular schmo,' Fogler adds. 'At his core, he's that very simple palooka, you know, a loveable guy. But as things go along, we realize he's really quite unique.' Jacob is also a catalyst for Newt's coming out of his shell. 'Newt's been out in the jungles and the wild and he really communicates better with creatures than he does with people,' explains Fogler. 'I basically teach him how to be a person with people. And Newt introduces me to this amazing, fantastic, magical world.'

'Jacob is just caught up in the mix, but has the warmest of hearts,' says Eddie Redmayne, 'and he grounds this thing. He's the eyes of the audience when he gets pulled into this world.'

'Jacob just loves making people happy,' notes Fogler. 'And he loves cooking and baking for them. You know, he may not be able to perform magic, but he can make a little pastry that'll knock your socks off. So he *is* magical.'

BILLYWIG 'INFESTATION' IN MANHATTAN

As Newt and Tina head toward Jacob's apartment to recover his case, he observes a Billywig zipping its way around the Manhattan streets, unusual as they originate in Australia. The Billywig is a fast-flying, electric sapphire-blue insect. Dried Billywig stings are useful in medicinal potions.

The Billywig has escaped Newt's case but not his notice. Billywigs appears to have two different flight modes, one resembling a dragonfly's and the second that of a helicopter. The animators looked at dragonflies and hummingbirds as reference. The final Billywig concept transformed the wings into a propeller. 'There was a drawing in a book of a helicopter bluebottle fly that we've made more hummingbird size,' says VFX supervisor Christian Manz. 'But it does helicopter around.' Flies, who clean their own legs, were also referenced, as the Billywig grooms itself as it hovers.

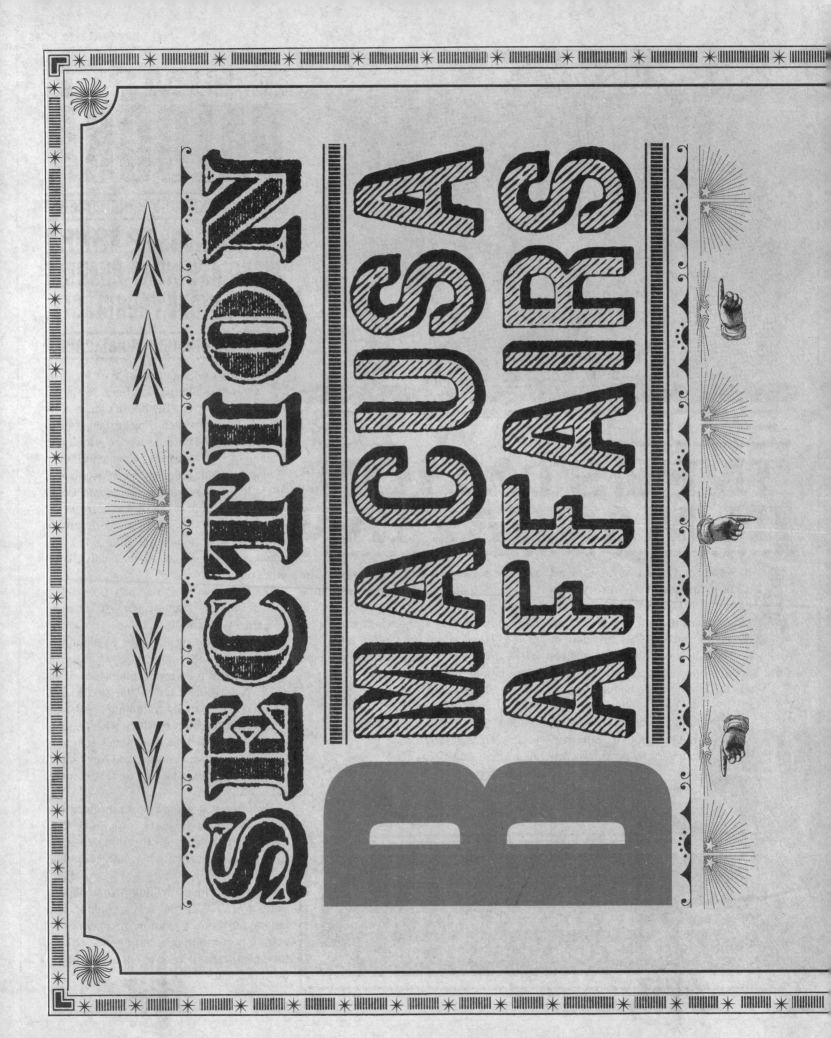

PERCIVAL GRAVES ASSERTS ATTACKS ARE NOT THE WORK OF GRINDELWALD

her message is one of intolerance,' Farrell observes. 'It's bigotry toward those of the wizarding ilk, so it's persecution. Samantha Morton's character is the person who is at the forefront of the movement to banish and to illegalize and to cast out, literally and physically, all wizards from New York.'

'IT'S BIGOTRY TOWARD THOSE OF THE WIZARDING ILK, SO IT'S PERSECUTION' – COLIN FARRELL

Farrell describes his character as 'very high up the command chain, there to investigate, control, and contain anyone or thing that is trifling with the Dark Arts, anything detrimental to wizardkind.' Graves would get involved if there were an attack against wizards from No-Majs as well, he confirms. 'But it's mostly the maintenance, the protection, and the upholding of the laws that we have set forth in North America to protect wizardkind. He's highly skilled. He's incredibly well-trained, and rather powerful. He would be very well respected. He would have information on inner sanctum facts and figures that not many people would have.

'And then, Eddie's character, Newt Scamander, comes into the frame and it unfolds from there.'

Despite the Magical Exposure Threat Level being raised, Percival Graves, Auror, Head of the Department of Magical Law Enforcement, and Director of Magical Security, asserts that the terrible attacks upon the city are not the work of Gellert Grindelwald, the dangerous Dark wizard who is currently at large. As Graves states: 'No human could do what this thing is capable of.'

'Graves is very proactively chasing this mystery that is running amok across New York City,' says actor Colin Farrell, who plays a character as enigmatic as this unknown force. 'We don't know at the start of the film whether it's a beast or a spirit or an entity or what it is. And before a war is provoked between No-Majs and wizardkind,

he wants to find this creature that's causing destruction and put it to rest.'

In addition to the unknown force that is causing destruction in the city, Graves is also mindful of the machinations of the New Salem Philanthropic Society. 'Mary Lou Barebone is militant in the way she demonstrates her will, not her message, because

SECRET ENFORCEMENT

Farrell cites the International Statute of Secrecy, whereby the magical community is living in hiding and secrecy, as 'almost a denial of our own existence in relation to No-Majs, in relation to common citizenry,' he states.

'Now there is something happening in New York that threatens to expose the world of magic and it's incumbent on me and President Picquery to figure out what's going on. Well, me, in a more active way on the streets.'

SO, WHO IS THIS CHILD, WHAT IS THEIR POWER, AND WHY DOES GRAVES SEEK IT?

THE VISION

And the No-Maj that Graves meets with is very unexpected: Credence Barebone, adopted son of the leader of the New Salem Philanthropic Society. Graves has asked Credence for his help in finding a very special child, a child with immense power. He has had a vision that Credence is the one who will gain this child's trust. Credence, he says, is the key.

Graves knows that Credence is interested in joining the wizarding world, though we haven't seen any evidence of magical ability. Later, Graves steps up the young man's hope by giving him a familiar, magical pendant with the symbol for the Deathly Hallows. This symbol represents three items that, when owned together, can make that wizard a master of death. When he finds the child, Graves tells Credence, all he needs to do is touch this symbol and he will come to him. Do this, says Graves, and he will be honoured among wizards. Forever.

So, who is this child, what is their power, and why does Graves seek it? Farrell worked with David Yates on the character's design. 'Graves is working in a place where he's worked for many years,' Farrell says, 'so if there was anything amiss, certainly significantly amiss in his behaviour, anything altered, there could be some very smart people in MACUSA who would send off alarm bells. Unbeknownst to those around him, Graves's political and social ideals are something that would be quite at odds or abrasive to those he's surrounded by daily. His true ideology is something that maybe wouldn't sit well in the hallowed halls of MACUSA.'

««« TAKE A TOUR OF MACUSA »»»

MACUSA'S BEAUTIFUL LOBBY

For those familiar, the entrance and exterior of MACUSA, housed in the No-Maj Woolworth Building downtown, might bear a slight resemblance to the architectural style of the Ministry of Magic; they are both grand and imposing. That is where the similarity ends.

'It's different to the Ministry of Magic in London in the sense that the same building is occupied in different dimensions,' says producer/screenwriter J.K. Rowling. 'So it's a Muggle building until you know the right way to get in. And then it changes and you're inside MACUSA.'

Rowling had visited New York City for inspiration for *Fantastic Beasts and Where to Find Them*, and was immediately taken with one of the city's most iconic landmarks. 'I had been to the Woolworth

> ## 'HORIZONTAL BANDS OF MARBLE IN TWO CONTRASTING COLOURS LED TO WHAT I THINK WAS A PRETTY STRONG IMAGE'
> ## – STUART CRAIG

Building and it was in my imagination,' says Rowling. 'When I was looking for the MACUSA headquarters, I thought of the Woolworth Building and looked at pictures.' At the top of the entrance arch to the building is a stone owl. 'It's just serendipity but sometimes you think, aah, that's why the owl's there,' says Rowling. '*Of course* that's why the owl's there.' Production designer Stuart Craig also visited the building and noticed the apt entrance. 'Jo had diligently researched her New York of that period. She must have seen that and gone, wow. *Eureka!* That building was constructed starting in 1905, and it's quite impressive to see up close.' To continue the serendipity, Craig had chosen the Gothic style as the guiding principle of the Harry Potter world, and the Woolworth Building is heavily decorated with gargoyles, salamanders (who, like phoenixes, survive fires), and trefoil arches in that mode.

At the time it was completed, in 1913, the Woolworth Building was the tallest building in the city, at seven hundred and fifty feet. 'And inside, it was not very interesting,' says Craig, 'so I had to think of something to do with it, to actually elevate it to something, well, ultimately magical.' Craig's solution? Eliminate the floors. 'There's one level above street level for a huge concourse, and then above that no floors at all. The lobby level is an open space, all the windows are exposed, and it's a vast cathedral of light.' This reminded Craig of the Sienna Cathedral in Italy, where the interior is banded in light and dark colour.'

THE SALEM MEMORIAL
REMEMBERING THOSE THAT LIT THE WAY

In the lobby of MACUSA stands a solemn memorial in remembrance of the Salem Witch Trials of 1692. Five larger-than-life bronze statues stand in a circle, four adults and one child, with sorrowful expressions. Their hands are bound in rope; their feet are bare.

Carmen Ejogo, who plays MACUSA's president, Seraphina Picquery, identifies the significance of the memorial as a reflection of the film's location: 'I think by setting it in the US, you bring to the fore what is a very recent history, and in some ways, America really hasn't moved on from those times. It really wasn't that long ago that the Salem Witch Trials actually did occur in this country, and that's very, very resonant in this community of wizards and witches. Having that as a backdrop has created an atmosphere and a world that feels even more palpable.'

Topping the columns beside the memorial are four large gold phoenixes, symbols of renewal. The statues and birds were sculpted by Bryn Court.

HAVE A COMPLEMENTARY WAND SHINE

'When you come up the stairs on the main concourse of MACUSA there is a wand polisher that operates like a shoe shine except he's not shining shoes, he's shining wands,' says Stuart Craig.

'[MACUSA] is almost like a lobby, like a station lobby,' says prop modeller Pierre Bohanna. 'Stuart wanted to put something in there that was in the style of the period. So he came up with the idea that was a play on a shoeshine stand, of someone having their wand polished. So you'd got a house-elf who is sitting by a big industrial polishing machine, grabbing wands and polishing them.'

A buffing wheel does the basic cleaning and polishing, getting the worst of the dirt out, and then a big, fluffy wheel of ostrich feathers finishes it off. 'The house-elf that operates the wand polishing machine puts the wand in his big feather buffers and sinks his arm in,' says Craig. 'When he withdraws it, his arm's shiny. That's actually not very magical, but it's charming. We do look all the time for little magical props that can give a little exotic touch to proceedings. It's a pleasing little thing and I like that rather a lot.'

GRAPHIC DESIGN OF ADVERT BY MINA LIMA

DIALLING IN TO THE MAGICAL EXPOSURE
THREAT LEVEL

Prominently hanging in MACUSA's lobby is a four-sided barometer-type dial that measures the risk of magic being revealed to No-Majs and keeps track of the number of witch hunts, Obliviations, and exposures. Created for the Department for Magical Security, the hand on the dial points to SEVERE: UNEXPLAINED ACTIVITY.

'It's almost like a station clock,' says graphic designer Miraphora Mina. 'It's about six feet across on each face, with a brass surround.' Mina and Eduardo Lima, Lead Graphic Designers, researched historical and vintage town hall clocks and other mechanical devices built in the Renaissance for its look. In addition to designing the face of the dial, the graphics team also drafted blueprints for the hands, which were given to the prop department and turned into a vectored file. With this, the modellers could then realize a 3-D prop. Working together, the prop and graphics departments created real working dials and controls for the mechanism.

MEET THE DEPARTMENTS
LUMOS ON:
THE WAND PERMIT OFFICE

One place to find employment at MACUSA is the Wand Permit Office. It's an important job, as all foreigners must have permits while in New York. This office is situated in a unique location in the MACUSA offices.

'How to be different and fresh [for MACUSA] was the challenge,' says Stuart Craig, 'and what I decided was that the basement floors were where the work is done. There's a wand registration office, a typing pool, and prison cells. The farther down you go, the more menial the work and the more dreadful the conditions.' In fact, in her screenplay, J.K. Rowling describes the Wand Permit Office as 'a cramped airless basement room. A painful contrast to the floors above. Clearly the place where utter no-hopers work.'

Anna Pinnock's set design was based on 'vast New York office corporations with floors of typist clerks that, typically in the '30s, used a system of vacuum suction pipes to transfer paperwork and messages throughout the building from floor to floor. In our world, there are no office workers and the typewriters magically type the replies to the Wand Applications, which are then magically folded and transformed into origami rats.'

Ninety-six typewriters grace the rows of desks. Miraphora Mina and Eduardo Lima created the unfolded, flat version of the Memorandum Rodentium, as well as thousands of flat applications, piles of unopened requests, permit replies, and permit envelopes, each individually glued into shape by hand. Two desks belong to the Goldstein sisters, Tina and Queenie, which reflect their different styles. Tina's desk is orderly and organized, with nary a paper out of place. Queenie's desk is a morass of permit papers, sweet packets, powder and blush, and even a sewing kit.

ABERNATHY AUTHORITY

The Wand Permit Office is lorded over by Abernathy, played by Kevin Guthrie. Abernathy is described as a 'pompous jobsworth' by Rowling, which is apparent in how he appears to treat Tina. But this wizard has several sides — he shows a nervous jittery one when he's near her sister, Queenie, and a definite obsequious side whenever he's near Percival Graves.

PERSONNEL PROFILES

THE GOLDSTEIN SISTERS

Porpentina Goldstein and her younger sister, Queenie, dispense and file permit applications for foreign wizards visiting New York City, as required. Tina joined MACUSA after her graduation from Ilvermorny School of Witchcraft and Wizardry, and worked as an Auror until she was discovered performing magic in front of a crowd of No-Majs — the Second Salemers, to be exact — causing a big scandal, as it entailed Obliviating the large group. Subsequent to this episode, Goldstein was demoted to become a Federal Wand Permit Officer.

'She loves the rules,' says Katherine Waterston, who plays Tina. 'She wants to stick by them. Tina has real skill as an Auror, but unfortunately, because she doesn't always handle situations as well as she hopes to, she's been demoted at work. She *is* good at her job, and if she can manage to get her career back on track, someday she might be respected in MACUSA. She's really proud to be part of it and dreams of succeeding there. But if someone's in trouble, she can't help herself. Ultimately, there was something more important to her, and that's why we find her stamping applications in the basement.'

And yet Tina did break the rules. 'I found it really touching that the only thing that will tempt

her to break away from the position she has is if someone is in trouble,' says Waterston. 'But by saving a No-Maj, she exposed herself as a magical person.'

Tina spots Newt Scamander as she surreptitiously spies on the Second Salemers in front of the bank. When she sees him take out his wand and Disapparate with Jacob, she knows that first, he's a wizard,

and second, something is going on that shouldn't be. 'She has good instincts,' Waterston says with a laugh. 'She's not a total disaster.'

When Newt and Tina meet, 'she's sort of had her wings clipped,' says Eddie Redmayne. 'But there's a strong work ethic to her and a desperation to prove herself.' So when confronted with Newt bringing his creatures into New York City, Tina has to make some hard decisions.

'With Newt and his case, the main problem is that it's a lot easier for witches and wizards to hide from the No-Maj world

than to hide magical creatures, especially ones that are on the loose in that community,' she explains. 'So that's the number one threat.' Waterston feels it's the same

'TINA LOVES THE RULES'
– KATHERINE WATERSTON

principal as if zoo animals, like a lion or an elephant, were let out in the middle of the city. 'It would be disastrous,' she explains. 'They plough things over, they break things, they could harm people. For most of the film, Tina is just imagining the worst-case scenario.'

The worst-case scenario includes exposure to the No-Maj community. 'In America, as it's established in the film, we've been taught that magical creatures are a bad thing,' Waterston continues. 'We should not have them at all, not in America and certainly not on the loose. She's almost panicked to get them back.' In her interactions with the beasts as they're tracked down and recovered, Tina gains a better appreciation for them and for Newt. 'So when push comes to shove, she again abandons the rule book and helps someone in trouble.'

LIVING WITH A LEGILIMENS

'THERE'S A LOVELY LACK OF SELF-CONSCIOUSNESS ABOUT HER'
– ALISON SUDOL

Queenie Goldstein, younger sister to Tina Goldstein, is a natural-born Legilimens. 'She has the ability to read minds,' explains Alison Sudol, who plays Queenie. 'And she can read people. It's a magic within her. It's not just reading somebody's thoughts,' she explains. 'She can read into someone's story; she can see people's goals. She can literally see everything you don't want to be seen, right down to your core.

'She's basically a complete and utter magical empath,' continues Sudol. 'So even though she's able to do magic with her wand, a lot of her magic is internal, which makes her a different type of wizard or witch.'

'Queenie is someone who is underestimated constantly,' says J.K. Rowling. This may be because her outward demeanour is so kind-hearted and carefree. She shines with both an inner and outer beauty. However, Queenie's skills as a Legilimens are not infallible, and can land her in trouble. 'She doesn't always draw the right conclusions from what she's reading.' Rowling explains, 'She still makes mistakes about people.'

Sudol describes Queenie as 'fun, joyful, and free-spirited . . . and [she] also has a stillness about her because she's always tuning in to people. As a Legilimens, Queenie's incredibly sensitive, of course. But she's also a playful spirit. I find her very aware and unaware of herself at the same time. She's thrilled to be on an adventure — things that would scare most people are just thrilling for her. She's quite an interesting character to play — very vivacious and lively, yet very centred and aware.

A SAD PAST LEADS TO STRONG SISTERS

Queenie and Tina have a very deep bond, having been orphaned at an early age. 'Tina and Queenie are each other's family,' says Alison Sudol. 'They're each other's everything.'

'The way that they relate to each other is very sweet,' says Katherine Waterston. 'And, of course, the thing that made them really close was something really, really painful.' The Goldstein sisters' parents died of dragon pox when they were children. 'You sort of feel their relationship more than you see it. I really thought it was an indication of Jo's skill and intelligence as a screenwriter to know that you don't always have to express the feeling on the line. I really love how they are the centre of each other's lives and take care of each other.'

> ## 'YOU DON'T NEED TO PROVE HOW MUCH YOU LOVE SOMEBODY IF YOU LOVE THEM ENOUGH'
> — ALISON SUDOL

'It's very easy for Queenie to just love Tina,' Sudol maintains. 'There's the kind of love that nothing can change between them is a really beautiful thing. You don't need to prove how much you love somebody if you love them enough, and that's how I feel with Tina and Queenie.'

One of the first scenes the actresses shot together was when Tina brings Jacob and Newt to their apartment and offers them dinner. 'What's so amazing and insane about working in film,' says Waterston, 'is that sometimes you've just met a person, and then you have to move around in a space together as though you do it every day. So we scrambled to figure out, well, "How

would they prepare the room together? Whose chores are whose?"' Queenie seems to be doing most if not all of the cooking. 'So I was setting the table with my wand,' Waterston continues. 'We developed a superstitious kind of salt-over-the-shoulder-toss thing, just to give the audience a sense of their life together.' The sisters also participate in some everyday and comfortable banter, in which Queenie chides Tina for having only a frankfurter for lunch, and Tina snaps back with a quick 'Don't read my mind.' Waterston describes it as 'a sort of witchy way that sisters engage with one another.

'Their world is very insulated and private,' she adds. 'They don't often have any guests so this is a total freak exception, which added another level to it. It was really fun to figure out how to show the private and the new experiences at the same time.'

Though her character is older, Katherine Waterston feels that they both parent each other at different times. 'And I'm a bit more the father and she's a bit more the mother. Queenie has a generous, maternal quality to her. She cooks beautiful, elaborate meals. And maybe, in their loneliness, they've fallen into that dynamic, where I'm trying to be the breadwinner, and she's doing the ironing. On one level it's a throwback relationship: they're the mother and the father they lost. Then, also, there are aspects to both of them that I think are underdeveloped, because they never really got to be kids. So, on another level, they're like two kids in their bunk bed, and maybe part of the journey in the film is just bringing them to their actual place in the world.'

SECTION C

WIZARDING HOME AND STYLE

HUNDREDS DRESS FOR CHILLY NEW YORK WINTER

COLLEEN ATWOOD WAS CHARGED WITH CREATING AN AUTHENTICITY TO THE TIME PERIOD BY DIRECTOR DAVID YATES.

'He wanted a real feeling of the frenetic energy of New York, and the feeling of somebody coming into that world from a different world,' says Atwood. 'A real feeling of the texture of the explosion that is New York — of all kinds of people from all over the world coming together and making a city.'

Atwood was extremely excited to costume a movie set in the 1920s. 'It was a crazy time of excess in all ways. Prohibition was going on, but people drank and people partied — it was intense. The intensity of the era appealed to me. It was the beginning of jazz as a popular form of music. I love the hair and the makeup and the style.'

She also finds dressing the extras a fun part of the design process. 'You can do stuff on crowds that you cannot do on the principals; it's not like you're creating a character you're looking at scene after scene. You have a little more freedom. It can be like a big splash or a quick pop or something different than what you're doing with the principals.'

EXTRA DRESSING

For Atwood, the background extras are as important as the main cast. 'To me, the background is part of the story and I care about them, especially in a story like this. They're the palette that sets the tone for the principals and the world.'

SERAPHINA STYLE

DRESS LIKE MACUSA'S PRESIDENT

T he imposing Seraphina Picquery, president of the Magical Congress of the United States of America, exudes a powerful style in both her authority and attire. One of her most eye-catching outfits is the dress she wears during the assembly of the International Confederation of Wizards held in the Pentagram Chamber. Colleen Atwood describes the long, structured dress, with bell-shaped sleeves and hemline, emblazoned with a stylized thunderbird emblem, as Seraphina's 'major moment.'

For her day-to-day outfit, Picquery, played by Carmen Ejogo, wears a bureaucratically tailored, three-piece pinstriped suit of jacket, vest, and skirt. Atwood went through what she calls her 'process of discovery' for Picquery's costumes, especially for the final scenes when Picquery and her Aurors battle in the New York subway. 'I thought a dress was going to look strange when she's with the Aurors in their leather coats and trousers,' says the designer. 'So I made a version of a pant with a skirt in the front.' This complements but still sets her apart from the Auror outfits.

A PROCESS OF DISCOVERY

S triking features of the president's wardrobe are the headdresses Picquery wears. Early on, it was thought she was from a country in Africa. So Atwood put together some initial concepts by looking at West African headdresses, thinking, 'Oh, those are great.' Director David Yates heartily agreed with her when shown the idea. 'He said that would be amazing for Seraphina.' Atwood designed a business-like head-wrap for office and outside wear, but went to town on the headdress she wears in the Pentagram Chamber, with layer upon layer of gold-toned silk flowers.

In Ejogo's opinion, 'Colleen is an absolute genius. She knows what she wants, but she's also very open to hearing ideas and incorporating them; she's appreciative of the fact that actors potentially have something to contribute, too.' Ejogo wanted to emphasize her own left-handedness, 'So I thought perhaps stacked rings might be a trait of Seraphina's.' Atwood loved the idea, 'and before I knew it I was stacked up!' says Ejogo.

DRESS LIKE MACUSA'S DIRECTOR OF MAGICAL SECURITY

Severus Snape in the Harry Potter films, Farrell noted that he had no costume changes. 'I had one option: take off the coat or leave on the coat.'

AS HEAD OF MACUSA'S DEPARTMENT OF MAGICAL LAW ENFORCEMENT, RENOWNED AUROR, AND DIRECTOR OF MAGICAL SECURITY — ESSENTIALLY PRESIDENT PICQUERY'S RIGHT-HAND MAN — PERCIVAL GRAVES DRESSES FOR HIS POSITION AND HIS POWER.

'Percival Graves is the ultimate wizard,' says Colleen Atwood, 'so I wanted to take his wardrobe to a level of twenties elegance with a touch of glamour and fantasy.' Atwood wanted to empower him in some way, and so exaggerated things on him. 'I gave him huge spat boots and a bigger shoulder. And then I wanted to do a slightly elegant, dandy thing with waistcoat, collar, and suspenders.'

Atwood used a cashmere/Lurex blend. Lurex, as a fabric, is woven with metallic threads that give it a subtle sheen. 'So it had a bit of shine to it, but not enough that it looked blingy. Just enough to give

it a kind of squinty quality that I really like.'

'My costume was *cool*,' says Colin Farrell. 'A great big long coat that just bordered on

being a cloak. Not quite a cloak but nearly a cloak.' Atwood dressed him in what she called a 'clerical vibe,' in black and white. 'Like my hair,' jokes Farrell. 'But it had that kind of priestly feel to it that it was more than just clothing. It was a representation of the structure of his life and his own ideologies and set of beliefs and his discipline.' Similar to

GRAVES'S GARB

Graves wears what might be considered the closest thing to the robes we are familiar with seeing in the Harry Potter films. 'I didn't think I needed to do a robe for this interpretation. But I wanted his coat to have sweep,' Atwood says. 'I talked to him about what he was going to do in the film, how he was going to move in it, and so designed a coat that was very sleek, but still had a kick to the hem.'

FASHION REPORT:

The International Confederation of Wizards, which meets in the Pentagram Chamber of the Magical Congress of the United States of America, features magical ambassadors and administrators from countries around the world.

There were occasions in the Harry Potter films when we saw the wider world of wizards working at the Ministry, especially in *Harry Potter and the Order of the Phoenix*, but most of the costumes resonated with the Dickensian look established by Judianna Makovsky in *Harry Potter and the Philosopher's Stone*. The meeting of the international wizarding community in the Pentagram Chamber in *Fantastic Beasts and Where to Find Them* provided an opportunity to display an even more multifaceted view of the wizarding world.

'There is a scene that takes place in an inner chamber that is kind of like the House of Lords,' says Colin Farrell. 'And there must have been two hundred actors and extras and day players who were representatives from all over the world there, all in different costumes. Wizards from Hungary and wizards from Mongolia, Russia, Thailand, Pakistan, and Ireland. It was amazing because they all wore the culturally relevant garb that people from the country they were representing would be wearing, but with a little wizarding flourish, so it's just a little bit more bizarre. Colleen and all the wardrobe and hair and makeup folks did an extraordinary job.'

'I'm very happy with its success because I was afraid [David Yates and David Heyman] might pull back on it, but they embraced it,' Atwood says. 'I had pretty free rein. They definitely looked at everything and considered everything carefully, especially the main people, but they loved the MACUSA look right off the bat.'

'Colleen has this bonkers imagination,' says David Heyman with a smile, 'but she is also a real student of design and the history of costume, and I think she is able to combine the eccentric and the extraordinary with great elegance, taste, and relatability.'

David Yates extends the compliment with his own description: 'Colleen Atwood: designer extraordinaire, extraordinarily handsome, strong personality, great conviction, bold vision, and an absolute pleasure to work with.'

WHAT THEY WORE AT THE EMERGENCY MEETING OF THE INTERNATIONAL CONFEDERATION OF WIZARDS

FIELD WEAR FLAIR: THAT COAT

Magizoologist Newt Scamander doesn't wear a uniform, but he does wear a very distinct coat.

When costume designer Colleen Atwood begins to design a costume, she thinks about what she calls the 'off the page character.' 'The character comes from somewhere,' she explains. '[Newt's] been living in the wilderness. Maybe he adapts everything to what he needs in his own world, but he does have to blend with the real world.' To evoke this idea, Atwood used the silhouette of the 1920s, but made his clothes slightly mismatched and a bit ill-fitting, to give a feeling of quirkiness to the character.

Her next consideration was his colour palette. 'There are a lot of browns in the period. I wanted to separate him out, but, again, still have him work within the world of the period, so I chose a deep, sort of dirty peacock blue for his coat. And the colour has the vibe of some of his fantastical creatures.' Atwood had the material she used for Newt's coat in her storeroom for years before she finally used it. Twelve duplicate coats were manufactured.

> 'NEWT'S COAT IS A MASSIVE ELEMENT OF NEWT'S CHARACTER'
> – EDDIE REDMAYNE

POCKET POTENTIAL

Among Atwood's early concepts for the coat was the thought that perhaps Newt's coat had pockets inside and out. 'He would keep pets in there,' Atwood explains. 'And keep some of his medicines and his cures around him.' So Atwood based it on another profession that required a specialized coat. 'I did research on magician's coats and how they had all their secret pockets — that was my starting point for the interior of his coat. When it came to screen time, we see very little of it, but it was fun to develop with Eddie and play with it.'

HE WEARS IT WELL

'Newt's outfit is well-worn and well-loved,' says textile artist Matt Reitsma. 'He's an adventurer, he's been all over the world, he's been everywhere. So his clothes really needed to sit on his body.' As part of 'breaking down' Newt's costume, the pieces were steamed many times to get the fibres to sink in. 'Colleen is also really fond of "waxing" fabrics, to give them a suppleness and sheen; I think she's one of the only people that uses that technique,' Reitsma adds. 'It gives an oddly luminous look, to wools in particular, which is perfect for Eddie's character because he wears a very heavy wool coat. It's really amazing to see it on him, and see how well it suits his character.'

'Newt's coat, in a way, is a massive element of Newt's character,' expresses Redmayne, 'which Colleen and I explored. One of the things that we loved is that he really only wears one outfit the whole way through the film. But as the story goes on, the collar pops and the trousers get tucked into his boots. He goes from having a slightly eccentric nerdy quality to him that turns into a slightly more, "Oh, he looks a bit more like an adventurer" by the end of the film.'

GOLDSTEIN GARB:
WHAT WITCHES WEAR IN THE WAND PERMIT OFFICE

Can two sisters have completely different approaches to fashion? They can, and yet both can be the Kneazle's meow.

'Tina Goldstein is one of those quirky girls who's a little bit gawky, a little bit not quite *there* in her body and just a little bit off in her costume,' says Colleen Atwood. The costume designer also describes her as a modern girl, and made the decision to put her in trousers, which was not very common for women in the period but did happen. Atwood strongly considered Tina's job, or her former job, when creating her outfits. 'She had been thrown out of a certain world that she'd been part of, so she was part of that world but not anymore. So Tina wore elements of what the Aurors wore, hence the trousers. Also, she was doing a "private eye" thing, like stealth spying work, so I gave her a trench coat with a really big collar she could tuck her head behind.

'Queenie uses her magic in a different way,' she continues. 'She's got a different energy to Tina altogether and I wanted to dress her in a different way.' To demonstrate this difference, Atwood dressed Queenie in soft, silky fabrics in warm greys and approachable light roses and pinks. 'Queenie was a lot of fun,' admits Atwood. 'I had a coat woven for her. The weaver told me afterward that it took thirty thousand feet of thread to make that coat. It's all silk thread, all different ombre colours of peach, which I thought looked like a sunset or a sunrise. There was an element of air and light to it, which I liked for Queenie.' Atwood also designed some underclothes for Queenie. 'Just a kind of take on a witch's dress, but with a 1920s slant and a bit of fun to it.'

NO-MAJ STYLE: KOWALSKI COUTURE

Striving to qualify for a bank loan to fund his dream of a bakery, No-Maj Jacob Kowalski puts on his best attire to create a good first impression.

'Jacob is what you'd describe as a schlub, back in the day,' says Colleen Atwood. 'We meet him trying to get a loan from a bank and in contrast to most men of that era, even if they were not of wealth, they pulled themselves together and had some sort of suit that looked presentable. Well, Jacob had so little money that he had to buy used clothes, but because of his shape, they don't quite fit the way they should.' Atwood chose softer fabrics than normal for the period, as they would easily sag. There are little mends and patches on the threadbare pieces, and his vest buttons don't match. 'Jacob's suit is creased and wrinkled and shiny and overwrought,' says textile artist Matt Reitsma, who 'broke down' Dan Fogler's outfit. 'It was really fun to take a finely tailored garment and give it character, really make it his.' 'Colleen is brilliant,' says Dan Fogler. 'She makes you look really good. You look good in her clothes, they look good on screen, and she also uses them to tell the story.'

Cupid's Corner

REMEMBER RAPPAPORT'S LAW

'HE IS LOYAL, AND HE LOVES TO BAKE AND SHE LOVES TO COOK. HE MAKES HER LAUGH. HE RESPECTS HER. THERE'S A REAL SENSE OF GOOD OLD-FASHIONED TRUE GENTLEMANLINESS.'

'Queenie loves Jacob,' says Alison Sudol, 'because she's able to see into him like she can, she sees how good he is through and through. It's a lovely dynamic between the two of them that he can't hide from her — but he has nothing to hide, because even when he says something that he doesn't mean to, it's still great.'

'Queenie is just an angel,' says Dan Fogler. 'The two of them start to fall in love and it gives Jacob a real reason to want to stick around.'

Unfortunately, the laws at the time, specifically Rappaport's Law, seek to prevent them being together. 'The climate is that the wizarding community doesn't want No-Majs mixing with the wizards and the witches,' Fogler explains. 'There are strict laws, especially in New York, that we're not allowed to be together. It's forbidden. They think if it does happen everything will just unravel. It also mirrors the racism of the time,' Fogler continues. 'It's really quite beautiful how Jo [Rowling] parallels the cultural conundrums.'

These laws are not unknown to those outside New York, and even America. Newt

Scamander and Tina Goldstein discuss this issue almost immediately when she asks him what he knows about her wizarding community in America. He calls the law

about not having relations with non-magical people 'backward' and considers not being able to marry or even befriend No-Majs as 'mildly absurd.'

SHARING THE SAME DIFFERENCES

Alison Sudol reveals the catch in this 'us and them' mentality between wizards and No-Majs. 'They're always intermingling. So it's this strange sense of living with people you're fascinated by, but you're not allowed to get close to, because otherwise it could jeopardize everything. There's this fascination, and a realization that humanity can access: Even though we may be a little bit different — we can cook dinner with our wands — there is still something very much in common between the two worlds.'

DO OPPOSITES ATTRACT?

As they work to recover the beasts, Tina Goldstein and Newt Scamander develop a mutual respect for each other — and maybe a little bit more.

'It's wonderful how, throughout the film, they reveal little bits of their past and certainly reveal a great deal of their character to each other,' says Katherine Waterston. 'As things are when you first meet someone, you get a very general sense of who they are. My sense of who Newt is at the beginning is that he's dangerous and untrustworthy, and kind of cute, too,' she says with a laugh. 'As the relationship evolves, she sees what's motivating him and why he is the way he is.' Waterston found parallels between their characters which could encourage a deeper relationship. 'They are both very passionate about what they do. They are both a little stunted, not very good at expressing themselves. And then you start to see the reasons why they have become that way. He's very isolated in his work. She's become the parent to her sister, Queenie, because they lost their parents when they were young. So they're these two people who really haven't had much time to have a *good* time.' Their personalities are even more apparent in contrast to Jacob's and Queenie's. 'They're much freer,' Waterston continues, 'and it's in that contrast that you see how trapped they are. The moments where a little bit of who they really are gets to come out, it's really exciting. And as the film goes on, that starts to happen more and more.'

Recipe Corner:
Queenie Goldstein's Baked Apple Strudel

One of Queenie Goldstein's favourite pastimes is cooking, and so Miraphora Mina and Eduardo Lima, heads of the graphic department, populated the Goldstein apartment with cookbooks, including one on how to cook like a No-Maj, called *Franks and Human Beans* (published by ML Books). The book just happens to have a recipe for one of Jacob Kowalski's favourite desserts: apple strudel. Queenie prepares the pastry when Jacob and Newt Scamander are brought home by her sister, Tina. Mina and Lima even provided the labels for the flour and sugar used in the recipe.

Carrots and potatoes are sliced before dropping into a simmering stew, which is eventually ladled into the china bowls for the main meal. Plates and bowls rise out of cupboards to join forks, knives, and even candles that have flown around the room before setting the table. Apples are peeled and sliced, then combined with raisins and spices before being wrapped in several layers of rolled dough. Dough roses twist in the air before winding up on the pastry, accompanied by leaves that land like butterflies, all sprinkled with a generous helping of powdered sugar.

The animators made sure that the strudel was cooked to a crispy brown before landing in the centre of the table. The shot contained texturing and shading that would mimic the appearance of the strudel cooking while it's floating through the air, and like most baked goods, had it shrink down a little while it cooks, all to Jacob's amazement.

For Alison Sudol, that scene was a pinnacle of her shooting experience. 'I think the moment when we all first meet in the apartment, with the cooking scene and then sitting at the dinner table, still stands out as one of the most special moments of the film, because it was just such a wonderful and challenging ballet that we managed to work our way through.' Alison Sudol and Katherine Waterston discussed and practised the scene, in order to make sure there was a system and order to their motions. 'Also, it was this moment where we were all four forced together in the room working together, getting to know each other,' Sudol continues. 'And the apartment was so beautiful, and the lighting was so beautiful, and the scene was so warm. It was as magical as it looks.'

SECTION

1

DARK ARTS AND ENTERTAINMENT

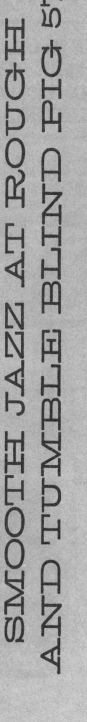

ARCHITECTURE
NEW YORK CITY: A MAGICAL METROPOLIS

'IT'S LIKE A CHAMPAGNE BOTTLE BEING SHAKEN UP,' SAYS DIRECTOR DAVID YATES. 'IT'S FIZZY, AND IT'S CRAZY, AND IT'S ALIVE, AND IT'S ECLECTIC. IT'S A WORLD FULL OF PEOPLE WHO HAVE DREAMS AND ASPIRATIONS. NEW YORK IN 1926 IS AN EXTRAORDINARY PLACE.'

'I had this idea that Newt went to New York, and it amused me, it tickled me, because in my imagination he was so not an urban person,' says screenwriter J.K. Rowling. 'Newt's in an alien environment on so many levels.'

'1926 was an incredible time,' says David Heyman, 'with enormous cultural changes and modern skyscrapers being constructed alongside more classical architecture. What's fun about *Fantastic Beasts* is that we have an opportunity to bring the audience into an entirely different time and place in the wizarding world, but [production designer] Stuart Craig's brilliant designs keep everything — even the most magical of settings — grounded in reality.'

'New York's probably the biggest creature we had to design in the movie,' says visual effects supervisor Christian Manz. 'And I think, much like the creatures, we wanted to keep it very grounded, and make

you believe that you really are experiencing what it was like to be in New York, the buzz of New York, in that time.'

Stuart Craig and his team pored through photos and live footage from the 1920s, as well as major motion pictures set at that time. 'It's very interesting in terms of its historical perspective. New York City in 1926 was huge and prosperous, before the big Wall Street Crash of 1929.' From a design aspect, Craig appreciated that most of the buildings of the period had a much unified, specific colour scheme. 'The bricks and brownstone buildings have the same colour,' says Craig. 'There was a nice cohesive

'NEW YORK'S PROBABLY THE BIGGEST CREATURE WE HAD TO DESIGN' – CHRISTIAN MANZ

unity to the landscape that I enjoyed very much.'

In order to visualize the most efficient way to lay out the various neighbourhoods in the city, Craig started with a model of the complex of New York streets. 'It was very deliberately designed to give us a variety of tenement buildings in the Lower East Side,

where Jacob lives. The middle section is based on Tribeca [below Soho], because it was just really interesting architecture. There's a lot of cast iron in Tribeca, it doesn't exist everywhere in New York, but its crisp architectural detail is very pleasing to anybody interested in architecture, like me.' The basic form of the layout is a T. 'At the top of the T was the

bank, hotel, and the MACUSA building itself.' Another section contains the brownstone where Tina and Queenie live. We had an appropriate neighbourhood for each of the main characters.'

'New York is an ecosystem of its own,' says director David Yates. 'In our movie we cover the very wealthiest in society, the ambitious, the moneyed, the political, and then we look at those in the tenements. They've escaped from poverty in Europe and they've come to build a new life and it's teeming over one another. So we have the whole of New York in that period: an extraordinary alive place, and a precarious place to let some beasts out into.'

ART GRAPHIC TEAM DRAWN TO CITY

Graphic artists Miraphora Mina, who began on *Harry Potter and the Philosopher's Stone*, and Eduardo Lima, who joined the graphics department on *Harry Potter and the Chamber of Secrets*, provided textbooks, newspapers, magazines, and the Marauders Map of Hogwarts for the films. They also worked closely with the prop and set decoration departments, creating drink and food labels, Ministry of Magic paperwork, Weasleys' Wizard Wheezes packaging, and endless ephemera that gave detail and depth to the on-screen wizarding world. Fortunately, the team returned to bring their considerable talent and eye for detail to *Fantastic Beasts and Where to Find Them*.

The designers began work six months before shooting started, researching typography and art styles of the 1920s at historical archives in New York, as well as developing how the era would transfer into the wizarding world. A new wizarding government entity, MACUSA required its own unique bureaucratic forms, including wand permits, memos that turned into origami rats, and a clock displaying the ever-changing threat level against witches and wizards.

Mina and Lima take their involvement down to the tiniest feature. 'Newt's passport, all his little belongings, and all the medicine labels he uses to treat the beasts, we had to do one by one,' says Eduardo Lima.

'We needed to ask Jo [Rowling] about those things,' Mina adds, 'like what's his birthday, where was he born, all those details that you might not see. We have to create the integrity of a piece.

'I guess our job is to try and understand how you got to that

'IT'S NOT ABOUT THAT MOMENT, IT'S ABOUT WHAT HAPPENED BEFORE THAT'
– MIRAPHORA MINA

moment that you're seeing for one second onscreen,' Mina continues. 'So it's not about that moment, it's about what happened before that. To make the viewer believe that it was always like that, or that there is a reason for it to be like that. Sometimes,' Mina says with a smile, 'we'll have quite ridiculous conversations about how something should be. That backstory is not in the books or in the film, but you need to know what it took to get there.'

Lips That Charm!

THE BLIND PIG

Enchanting. Beguiling. Alluring.

TRANSFIGURATION TODAY
EDITION 2579 · THE MAGAZINE THAT CHANGES LIVES

ESSAYS
ILVERMORNY SCHOLARS' VANISHMENT REPORT

LYCANTHROPY v. WEREWOLFERY
Arsenius Jigger explains
WHICH LOCUTION BETTER DESCRIBES THE WEREWOLVES?

THE SCIENTIFIC ASPECTS OF HUMAN TRANSFIGURATION
by EMERIC SWITCH Pg.12

HOW TO IDENTIFY UNREGISTERED and UNLAWFUL ANIMAGI

Continues on.......Pg.4

Join the debate:
THE PROS & CONS OF EXPOXIMISING Pg.9

THE PROCESS UNRAVELLED schematics on page 23

Continues on.... Pg.17

NEW CONTRIBUTOR
ALBUS DUMBLEDORE
IS VANISHING WITHOUT A TRACE POSSIBLE?
MY VIEW ON METAMORPHMAGUS Pg.21

DESIGN

SECOND SALEMERS SIGN SIGNALS STRONG STATEMENT

The emblem of the New Salem Philanthropic Society has a background of flames flickering below a pair of hands breaking a wand. 'It was referenced in the script as being a broken wand with a dove,' says Miraphora Mina. Mina and Eduardo Lima discussed the look of the banner with David Yates and David Heyman. 'They wanted it to be stronger and more aggressive than a dove,' recalls Lima. 'So we gave them the suggestion to have arms breaking the wand.' This was a reference to Mary Lou Barebone's mission to stamp out magic. 'Mary Lou was fun to design props for, because she's so evil and horrible,' says Lima. 'Never forget that we need to save America from witches!'

FINAL APPEARANCE OF CIRCUS ARCANUS
DEC 13

Look closely in the film, and you will see that the Circus Arcanus will give their final spectacular show in New York City at 8.00 p.m. on 13 December, 1926. The Circus opened here on 29 November, and will leave for Europe following their final performance.

HOGWARTS PROFESSOR JOINS TRANSFIGURATION TODAY

According to *Transfiguration Today*, one of the many props created by the graphics team, Hogwarts professor Albus Dumbledore has become a contributor. His first column explains his view on Metamorphmagus: 'Is Vanishing Without A Trace Possible?' Author Emeric Switch has contributed an article to same: 'The Scientific Aspects of Human Transfiguration.'

DO YOU WANT TO BE A MAGIZOOLOGIST?

THEN THINK INSIDE THE BOX

In order to transport his collection of beasts, Magizoologist Newt Scamander created a series of environments that can be hidden in an innocent-looking leather case. Each beast has its own area, but there can be interaction between the beasts as these areas are not walled-off, separate containers, except for some of the bigger beasts.

'Newt's case is an extraordinary world,' says director David Yates. 'It's immersive and fantastical and funny and scary, and I loved the fact that it's all contained in something you could take on a plane or a train.' Ever since the latch on his case popped open while Newt was in US Customs, anticipation kept growing for the time when what was inside the case would be revealed. 'This *is* the heart of the movie,' says Christian Manz.

OUT INTO THE CASE

Eddie Redmayne describes the interior of the case as a reflection of Newt's character. 'There's an almost biological element to it,' he explains. 'You see the passion he has for these different animals and plants. You see the drawings he's done. It's his character in physical terms. And once you descend into his shed and then out into the world of the case, well, it really pushes imagination to new extremes.'

The first challenge for the production designer was that 'there were no rules, and no precedents.' 'We went through many,

> 'NEWT'S CASE IS HIS WORLD. IT'S HIS HAVEN, REALLY. 'THE SET THAT STUART HAD BUILT WAS EVERYTHING I COULD HAVE DREAMED OF AND MORE.' – EDDIE REDMAYNE.

many iterations of what it might be,' Craig admits. 'We talked about cabinets with dioramas, or possibly a Victorian-type museum, but those wouldn't do for live animals.' Neither would a zoo-type approach as Craig knew that Newt would not keep his beasts in cages. 'Newt is about the preservation of these creatures,' he says, 'and their happiness in their respective environments. He would have made these magical environments himself.'

Once inside, each beast had its own created environment. 'The idea became to show as wide a variety of creatures as possible in their natural habitats,' says Christian Manz. 'We planned to have Newt walk through a safari that we would shoot on location. When J.K. Rowling saw our presentation, she suggested it would take a wizard more powerful than Voldemort to have created it. So, we had to pare our ideas back and came up with more of a "Heath Robinson" approach in which Newt had patched each creature's pen together.' During the First World War, Robinson was known for creating humorous cartoons of madcap secret weapons created with common household items as well as illustrations depicting the American Expeditionary Force in France.

'The key was that this whole place is made by Newt himself, so it has a homemade, DIY look,' says Craig. 'But as you step inside what looks like a theatrical backdrop of scenery,

CONTINUED ON PAGE 51

WILD WILD INFLUENCES

Two strong influences aided the visual development of the beasts' areas, one being the dioramas at the American Museum of Natural History that illustrate animals' habitats. 'They're painted to look real, but when you're standing looking at them you're aware that they're not,' says Dermot Power, 'but you're feeling the reality of it.'

Another key reference Power used were images of the nineteenth-century Buffalo Bill's Wild West shows. 'They used painted backdrops, and you could tell in these photos they had really made an effort to make it look like a realistic landscape, but then had hung it up really carelessly.' Real painted backdrops were created by Marcus Williams, the film's scenic artist, to establish the correct aesthetic and serve as the starting point for the animated environments.

Dermot Power's impression of Newt's character is that 'he loves the animals so much he's gone to great trouble to create these worlds for them, but he doesn't see his career as being the greatest 'world creator.' His career is taking care of animals. So if the environments are a bit shaky, he just makes sure they work. If things break off he'll patch it. He's just pleased that the animals are happy in the worlds he's created.'

THE SHED

One of our early decisions was to give Newt a shed in this magical space,' says Stuart Craig. 'He's more comfortable there than with his fellow human beings.' The tall, skinny shed houses his medicines and potions, and all other equipment needed to capture and care for the creatures. 'Being solitary seems to be a necessary part of his life at times,' says Craig, 'so we gave him the shed. He has a workbench. He has a bed under the bench. He has a stove, an armchair. It is a great place for a man like Newt to be alone.'

Set designer Anna Pinnock considered the shed an opportunity to convey the world of Newt and his personality through the space and its contents. 'We wanted to suggest Newt had travelled extensively in both the real and fantasy worlds,' she explains, 'so we introduced ethnic pieces, agricultural and zoological tools, and a great variety of unusual containers and receptacles. Every item had to have a function or purpose. We found Oriental medicine cabinets and chests that we fixed to the wall facing the door in a patchwork design from top to bottom.' The prop making team enhanced the sourced items as well as creating new ones, and the graphic artists added labels, research notes, and wall charts.

The room also includes a photograph of Leta Lestrange, someone who was once very special to Newt.

THE SWOOPING EVIL

There is one creature Newt keeps close: the Swooping Evil, a designation the Magizoologist doesn't consider the friendliest of names. Newt has been studying him; he has a theory that the Swooping Evil's venom could be useful if properly diluted, to remove bad memories. Its luminous venom is extracted by squeezing on its cocoon-like case; the liquid is collected in a glass vial.

'My inner nine-year-old is obsessed with the Swooping Evil,' says Eddie Redmayne. 'He's like this spiky ball with a thread that hangs down from Newt's finger. When you spin him out, almost like a yo-yo, he unfurls into this terrifying creature.'

The Swooping Evil bears a similarity to a large butterfly or a prehistoric manta ray, with cape-like green wings and a magnificent cobalt-blue underside. Its skeletal head resembles a rodent's, with long, sabre-shaped canine teeth it uses as an encephalophage: an eater of brains. 'But Newt has complete control of it,' say visual effects supervisor Christian Manz. 'He calls it. It wraps back up and he puts it in his pocket. We were trying to work out, legitimately, how that would happen and make it believable. How do we get something that big into something small? And, of course, it's magic.

'We also wanted to see him use his creatures to get himself out of a scrape,' Manz adds, and Newt uses the Swooping Evil for defence several times through the story. The Swooping Evil can act as a distraction or shield during battle. It also has a strong-enough body to quickly, if close enough, carry a human from one spot to another.

PICKETT

THE BOWTRUCKLE

One of many delightful moments inside Newt's case takes place in the Bowtruckle environment. 'I love the Bowtruckle,' says J.K. Rowling. 'His name is Pickett. He doesn't quite fit in with his branch, which is the technical term for a lot of Bowtruckles. They're little twig-like creatures so I said you have a branch of Bowtruckles.'

A branch of Bowtruckles live inside Newt's case, consisting of Titus, Finn, Poppy, Marlow, and Tom. The sixth member of the branch is Pickett, who spends most of his time in Newt's breast pocket. 'Pickett may be my favourite creature' admits Eddie Redmayne. 'He's a bit of a loner within the family of Bowtruckles. He feels a bit bullied by his pals. He has attachment issues. So he keeps faking illness in order to hang out in my pocket.' And Newt indulges him.

Bowtruckles are also animator Pablo Grillo's favourite creatures. 'I don't even really know what they are but they're incredibly inviting.' The Bowtruckle went through almost two hundred iterations before its final look. 'Pickett's design had to communicate the fragility of the animal,'

Grillo explains. 'It had to echo Newt's fragility, in a way, without being weak. He's a courageous creature, there's a heart and a valour to this creature. Pickett is a bit of a social outcast like Newt, too.'

Bowtruckles have great value in spite of their size. 'He has this extraordinary quality of being incredibly agile, and can also pick locks,' says Redmayne. Pickett's ability will prove useful in helping Newt get out of several close calls with danger.

For rehearsals, Grillo's puppeteers brought Pickett to life in several ways. 'He lives in my pocket, but frequently comes up onto my shoulder,' says Redmayne. 'I started by having a puppeteer literally using a finger puppet to do it, feeling what that was like. Then they had a long rod with Pickett, made out of wire on the end. When we actually filmed he was not there, but by

[that time] you can play with him because you have a sense of him.'

'[Pickett's] very inexpressive facially,' says Grillo. 'To me these are the most exciting challenges, where you don't have to rely on a facial performance — it very much comes through the actions to reveal the intentions. With the right combination of shapes you can make him sad, proud, or be expressive for your heart to warm to him.'

'He didn't really have any facial animation, but he does blow a raspberry at one point,' says Christian Manz. 'In the end we added more shots of Pickett, as everyone just loved him.'

CONTINUED FROM PAGE 48

it becomes real. Crude at first, but magical and seemingly endless the farther you go in. It's a showcase for the creatures and they are, after all, the centre of the movie.'

GRAPHIC DESIGN OF ADVERT BY MINA LIMA

A DIFFERENT TYPE OF BEAST

As Jacob helps Newt feed his beasts within the case, he hears 'a kind of icy cry' coming from behind a billowing curtain. Following the sound, he finds himself in a snowscape, where a contained black mass is suspended in midair. The mass emits a disturbed, restless energy. Newt sharply tells him to step back from it, and gives him a curt answer of what it is: an Obscurus.

'The Obscurus is a really wonderful idea that Jo came up with,' explains David Yates. 'When a child is prohibited from developing their magic in a healthy, normal, organic, regular way, this dark energy can develop, and can suddenly get out of control, wreaking havoc and being quite dangerous.'

Children who have repressed their magical abilities, typically because of trauma or persecution, are called Obscurials. By doing so, they develop a parasitic Dark force — the Obscurus — that is unstable and uncontrollable, attacking

and then vanishing. Obscurials rarely live past the age of ten, and it's learned that the Obscurus Newt has in his case was separated from an eight-year-old Sudanese girl who then died. America hasn't been aware of any Obscurials in the country for two hundred years.

The Obscurus in Newt's case is enclosed. 'I was asked to show the Obscurus trapped in a box or tablet shape,' says Dermot Power, 'and liked the thought of two very different ideas colliding: the rigid square box and the swirling, almost liquid, force that yearns to be released.' Other studies included an image of a young girl suffering from her repressed magic, bound by a rectangular shell to illustrate the anguish of this tormented soul; and an organic mass 'with a hint of what is kept inside. Power loved the challenge of capturing such a unique entity and worked hard to portray the look of an invisible being in a cloud of dust.'

ENTERTAINMENT

OUT ON THE TOWN: A NIGHT AT THE BLIND PIG

Whispered conversations, games of chance, and a fully stocked bar of Gigglewater, Lobe Blaster, and Firewhisky — that's what you'll find at The Blind Pig. This Greenwich Village watering hole welcomes all wizards and witches, goblins and giants, served by the long-time goblin staff.

To help Newt find his remaining creatures, Tina Goldstein brings him, and Jacob and Queenie, to The Blind Pig, a speakeasy owned by Gnarlak, who was one of Tina's informants when she was an Auror. Speakeasies in the 1920s were hidden or disguised places where alcohol was purchased during Prohibition. They could be elegant, swanky places or a dim, grimy hole-in-the-wall. The Blind Pig falls into the latter category. 'This is an underground situation, hence a vaulted ceiling,' says Stuart Craig. 'We got as much character into this complex of tunnels and caverns as we possibly could. It's absolutely dripping in nicotine stains and water running down the curved walls. Makes a pretty threatening environment.'

'It's a dive bar,' says Christian Manz. 'We had a great prep period coming up with the stuff David [Yates] wanted to see in there. We've got a goblin jazz band and jazz singer, a house-elf barman, and house-elf waiters. We've got lots of moving wanted posters everywhere, magical gambling going on, plus all the drinks. For me it's one of the moments in the film where you really feel the 1920s.'

Gnarlak, a cigar- smoking, wisecracking goblin, is played by actor Ron Perlman. 'It's his establishment,' says Perlman. 'It caters more to the seedy underbelly of the wizarding world; a few people in there have a price on their heads. A few people in there have uneasy deals that they've made with MACUSA in order to stay at large. It's a broad range of unsavoury types and Gnarlak is the most unsavoury of all of them, because he's the master of all he purveys. And he's rather deliciously weird.

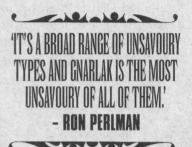

> **'IT'S A BROAD RANGE OF UNSAVOURY TYPES AND GNARLAK IS THE MOST UNSAVOURY OF ALL OF THEM.'**
> **– RON PERLMAN**

'A guy in Gnarlak's position just knows how to make deals with every strata, be it the highest stations in government or the lowest form of criminality and nefariousness,' Perlman continues. 'In order to preside over that world, he's gotta be among the smartest guys in the room. He uses intelligence for unsavoury ends, but he's pretty smart. He knows the playing field and he knows, like most con men, how to spot people's weaknesses and exploit them for his own benefit.'

SIX-FOOT ACTOR BECOMES FOUR-FOOT GOBLIN

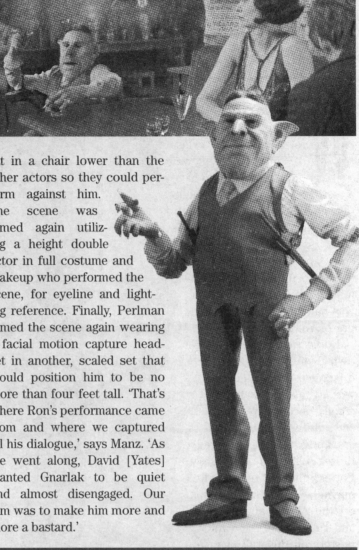

The goblins in the Harry Potter films were created by using prosthetics on the actors. 'Here we made them fully digital characters because we wanted to cast the right person and then not be bound by the human form,' says VFX supervisor Christian Manz. 'When Ron was cast, we moved into designing a character based upon him. We looked at lots of photos with period gangsters, some of the great pictures of people from the 1920s. There was a particular posture and a look that really gave you a sense of that character, and so that became key in conceiving what he looked like, but also keeping a lot of Ron in there as well, facially.'

Gnarlak came into being in several stages. First, as a CG character, Perlman offered more than ninety expressions that were captured in a photogrammetry session. Then, for filming the scenes, Perlman sat in a chair lower than the other actors so they could perform against him. The scene was filmed again utilizing a height double actor in full costume and makeup who performed the scene, for eyeline and lighting reference. Finally, Perlman filmed the scene again wearing a facial motion capture headset in another, scaled set that would position him to be no more than four feet tall. 'That's where Ron's performance came from and where we captured all his dialogue,' says Manz. 'As we went along, David [Yates] wanted Gnarlak to be quiet and almost disengaged. Our aim was to make him more and more a bastard.'

PICKETT'S PLIGHT

Newt realizes that he's going to need to bribe Gnarlak in order to get information, offering some Galleons, a Lunascope, and an Ashwinder egg. Nothing interests the goblin until he sees Pickett peeking out of Newt's pocket. 'The Bowtruckle has this extra added bonus feature of the ability to pick locks, so I mean, c'mon, it serves two purposes,' says Perlman. 'It's highly collectible *and* it's highly useful at the same time.' Newt's heartbreaking handover of Pickett gets him the information about his final missing beast. Fortunately, in the craziness of a raid by Aurors, Newt is able to retrieve him.

LIQUID GLEE

While Newt and Tina deal with Gnarlak, Queenie and Jacob get a chance to explore their relationship over a glass of Pinnock's Gigglewater. While trying to have a serious conversation, Jacob takes a shot and bursts out into, well, giggles. 'That was all Dan's idea,' says Katherine Waterston, 'and everybody thought it was so funny, they kept it in.' Pinnock's Gigglewater was named after the set decorator, Anna Pinnock.

Eddie Redmayne had his own gleeful moment, albeit offscreen. '[The Blind Pig] was my favourite set, principally because we got to see all the wanted posters, and I just flipping loved those posters in the Harry Potter films,' recalls Redmayne. When Gnarlak tips off the Aurors about Newt and Tina, two of the wanted posters on the wall change and display their images. 'So I got to film a moving wanted poster. It was a small but brilliant moment in my life.'

MUSIC REVIEW:

SMOOTH JAZZ
AT THE ROUGH AND TUMBLE
BLIND PIG

'IT'S JUST FULL OF CHARM AND BEAUTIFULLY IMAGINATIVE STRANGE DETAIL' – RON PERLMAN

The actor goes on to say: 'It's seedy but it's a place you wouldn't mind coming to have a drink. Picking up a broad; getting your swagger on. There's a come-hither quality to it. I don't care how cynical you are, you're going to come into this world wide-eyed and full of wonder. If you want a real good time, show up at The Blind Pig.'

The five-piece band playing at this popular speakeasy features drums, bass, piano, horns, and a fetching lead singer. 'For the instruments in the band, you will see the piano, at first sight, appears to be an upright piano,' says production designer Stuart Craig, 'but in fact it's an upright *grand* piano.' There's also a seven-foot-tall upright bass, played by a giant bass player; the remaining instruments are played by goblins. 'The pièce de résistance is the brass instrument,' says Craig, 'which is based on a sousaphone, but incorporates trumpet, bagpipe, and trombone.' Pierre Bohanna's team created these unique instruments. 'The brass player had a dozen different brass and wind instruments hanging around him, held together in a magical charge,' says Bohanna. 'We did it for real in the sense they were interconnected and on blacked-out stands so they floated in the air.'

THE SONG THE FEMALE GOBLIN SINGS HAS MUSIC BY MARIO GRIGOROV AND LYRICS BY J.K. ROWLING.

The band also boasts the first female goblin seen in any wizarding movie. An actress created her moves, which were recorded in motion capture, and then translated to the screen, accompanied by smoky images that illustrate the song. The musicians were also performed by actors. 'And Colleen Atwood made full costumes to scale,' says Christian Manz. These gave the animators an absolute reference of what they would need to recreate digitally.

WIZARDING WORLD NEWS

SECTION E

LATE EDITION

ANOTHER CREATURE FOUND – DIAMOND DISTRICT STORE DESTROYED

ICE HEIST

Newt is finally able to put the Niffler back in his case when he and Jacob spot it in the display window of a diamond shop. The Niffler attempts to fool them by remaining motionless, although diamond bracelets are slipping off his arm. 'The lovely thing about animals is their naivety,' says Pablo Grillo. 'They think if they stay still you can't see them.' Once again, the humour in the scene comes from Newt's and the Niffler's past 'and almost the respect Newt gives him for his skill. He admires it, but it's always getting them into problems.'

SLO MO APROPOS

A puppet was used as a stand-in for the Niffler for lighting and for scale, as well as for inter-action with the creature. 'The slow motion shot of the Niffler flying through the diamond district, with a nice 360-degree exploration of the space, is my favourite shot,' says Stéphane Nazé, VFX supervisor. 'Until that point, the audience are trying to catch glimpses of the Niffler — he's moving quickly, and always scuttling out of shot. When he's spinning through the air, we get to really enjoy him.'

ANIMALS ON THE LOOSE FROM
CENTRAL PARK

When a crew of Metropolitan police arrive in front of the store, it seems as if Newt and Jacob might be arrested. It doesn't help that they're covered in diamond jewellery. Then, to everyone's surprise, a lion strolls up the street. Using the distraction, Newt Apparates with Jacob to the Central Park Zoo. Arriving on the scene, they find many of the enclosures have been demolished by the amatory actions of the Erumpent that has escaped Newt's case.

THE ERUMPENT IS THE LARGEST BEAST NEWT SCAMANDER NEEDS TO RECOVER. TO COMPLICATE THE RETRIEVAL, SHE'S IN HEAT.

DISTURBING ACTIVITY IN CENTRAL PARK

'The Erumpent is a massive, almost indestructible creature,' says screenwriter J.K. Rowling, 'and David Yates injected it with a playfulness that I hadn't expected, and which is delightful.'

Erumpents can be described as a spectacular mashup of cow, rhino, hippopotamus, and bison. 'She's like a large grazer,' says senior animation supervisor Pablo Grillo. 'Doesn't have any more expressive potential than a cow. But through her actions you totally get her motives — she wants love, she's in heat, and the juxtaposition of that scale, that clumsiness, and that incredible desire fuses into something incredibly entertaining and charming and enjoyable and slapstick.'

'We wanted to give her a slight feminine quality without being too cartoony,' says visual effects supervisor Tim Burke. 'We found footage of a man in the Midwest who kept bison and had invited one into his house. It was amazing how this large beast suddenly moved cautiously, daintily, in the living room.'

FROM PUPPET TO PERFORMER

The puppeteers for *Fantastic Beasts and Where to Find Them* were headed by Robin Guiver, who starred in the original production of *War Horse* in London's West End. The idea of having an Erumpent puppet — which was almost seventeen feet tall, ten feet wide, and more than twenty feet long — was not just to give Eddie Redmayne an eyeline, but to give the actor and the director a physical character to play against. 'It's there to enable their performances. So David [Yates] has something he can direct very specifically,' Guiver explains. 'He can place it on the set. The camera can frame up on it. He'll be able to treat it as if he would an actor. He can dictate moves or emotions as he needs to, and he can look at the blocking of that mating dance, that ritual, as a very real event, rather than just asking Eddie to have to imagine all that. And there's something

CONTINUED ON PAGE **62**

CONTINUED FROM PAGE 61

there that has space, has mass, and hopefully should be able to provoke emotion as well.'

Having a physical representation of what would eventually become a digital beast was also a boon to the director of photography, Philippe Rousselot. 'It can be easy to frame on the actor and lose that sense of size,' explains Guiver. 'And when you put a character next to something this big, you can really get a sense of how small [he is] and how much danger he is in.'

Prop modeller Pierre Bohanna and his team created the puppet. 'Something of

that scale means that you have keep it incredibly lightweight,' he explains. The structure was made from carbon fibre tubes with a little bit of plastic tube on the outside. The Erumpent's head was fixed to its body, but had a cantilevered mechanism that allowed one of the puppeteers to give it movement. This Erumpent only weighed one hundred pounds. 'I was told that Big Bird was over a hundred and thirty pounds,' Bohanna adds. 'So I always have that in mind: if one man can cope with that, then that's a good way of working it out.'

'We had four people actually operating the puppet rig on that

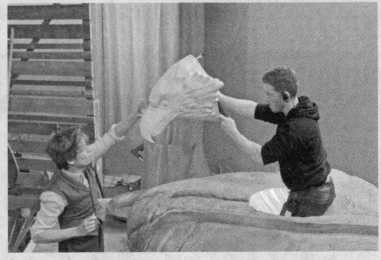

mating scene for every shot,' says Tim Burke. 'And before we even shot, they rehearsed that with Eddie, so they could get a

relationship down. For Eddie's character it was all about having that relationship with the actual creatures themselves.'

A NEW-MAJ LOVE INTEREST

case. 'Her body has its own momentum that is like steering a truck,' says Pablo Grillo. 'That can still be beautiful and graceful and charming and almost like a ballet. But animating that with the right weight and sense of jiggle that will sell the scale is always challenging.'

'There was also complex stuff from a technical standpoint, like the liquid sack on the Erumpent's forehead, that made her slightly more unusual than a normal creature,' says Christian Manz. 'That had to move and have internal lighting.' The prop department made her final three feet of horn in a hollow and translucent form so the electrical department could put a lighting effect inside that brightened as she got more and more excited. Fortunately, the explosive quality of the sack was handled digitally.

The Erumpent finds an even more interesting prospect in Jacob, who inadvertently gets splashed with a full bottle of Erumpent musk. 'We loved the idea of a relationship between Jacob and the Erumpent,' says David Yates. 'There's something about the Erumpent that's really beautiful and lovely. The fact that you can imbue this creature with its own desires and its own agenda I think just makes it a little bit realer in a way.'

The animators took as much care with the Erumpent as Newt did coaxing the beast into his

'I loved the Erumpent,' Redmayne reiterates. 'The more I read this script, the more I couldn't believe these animals and all the characteristics that Jo had thought up. The Erumpent is gigantic. The Erumpent is fast. And the Erumpent is in heat. When she gets out and Newt has to entice her back in with a mating dance, it involved one of the more humiliating moments in the film. It was weirdly exhausting.'

MAGIZOOLOGIST PERFORMS MATING DANCE

An Erumpent's size alone might seem to prohibit it from getting back into the case, but Newt has a few tricks available. First, he dabs himself with a drop of Erumpent musk. Then, he performs a mating dance. 'One great thing about J.K. Rowling's scripts is that descriptions are so intricate in detail,' says Eddie Redmayne. As Redmayne was reading through the script for the first time, 'There was this scene that just goes, "Newt performs mating dance." Two words have never filled me with so much sweat.' Redmayne Googled 'weird, random bird mating calls,' and as he developed the dance, made a few videos that he sent to the David Yates. 'They were the

most humiliating things you've ever seen in your life, and after waiting hours to hear his answer, his response would be, "I'm not sure it's quite seductive enough."'

Redmayne eventually came up with a call and movements designed to seduce the Erumpent. 'And we did have these amazing puppeteers, who would be doing sniggling noises and flirting, you know.'

Dan Fogler appreciated the care Eddie Redmayne took to showcase the Magizoologist's relationship with his beasts. 'When Newt is trying to coax the Erumpent back into the case by doing a very sexy dance for her, it's hysterical — but it's also science.'

'SEDUCING THE ERUMPENT WAS A MASSIVE HIGH POINT FOR ME' – EDDIE REDMAYNE

NEWT SCAMANDER FINDS TWO OF HIS BEASTS AT MIDTOWN DEPARTMENT STORE

An Occamy chick that escaped Newt Scamander's case is located in a midtown department store, being protected by another escaped creature, the Demiguise. 'Something invisible's been wreakin' havoc around Fifth Avenue,' Gnarlak, owner of The Blind Pig, told them. His words proved true when Newt and his companions, Tina, Jacob, and Queenie, saw a handbag levitate off a mannequin's hand in the store window and float down the department store's aisle. Once inside, they also discover the missing Occamy fledgling.

DAMAGE AT DEPARTMENT STORE

NO-MAJ MERCHANDISERS

THE INTERIORS OF THE SEQUENCE WERE FILMED IN LIVERPOOL, AT THE GRADE II-LISTED CUNARD BUILDING.

The department store where Newt finds his missing beasts was inspired by the upscale New York Fifth Avenue department store Bergdorf Goodman's. 'It is very elegant, with its glass top counters and use of art deco and mirrors, and rather beautiful,' says production designer Stuart Craig.

The interiors of the sequence were filmed in Liverpool, at the Grade II-listed Cunard Building. 'It lent itself very well,' says Craig. 'It has this size and was conceived and built with the confidence of New York in that period.' Set designer Anna Pinnock agreed with Craig's decision. 'So we set about building twelve twenty-eight-foot-long, double-ended, lozenge-shaped glass and wood cabinets that had to be filled with period merchandise,' she says.

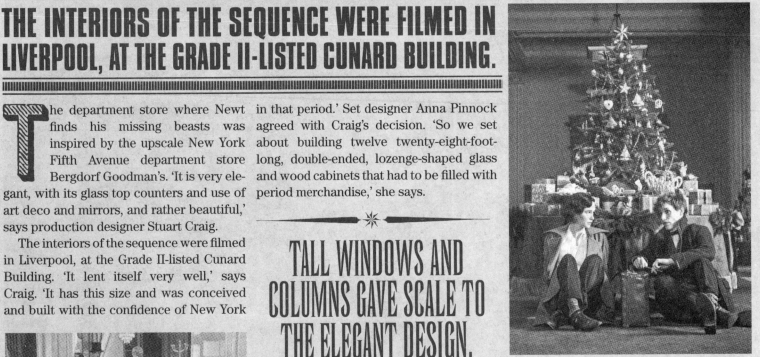

TALL WINDOWS AND COLUMNS GAVE SCALE TO THE ELEGANT DESIGN.

Specially made period-accurate male and female mannequins were created along with store window displays. The same space was used for both the ground and first floors, 'which meant double the amount of dressing,' explains Pinnock.

'We were also setting the scene at Christmas, which meant vast amounts of period decorations, two different looks and colours for each floor.' The storeroom was stocked with boxes stacked in a towering fashion, each box individually labelled and given delivery instructions by the graphics department.

THE OCCAMY: ONE SIZE DOES NOT FIT ALL

J.K. Rowling remembers being told in her youth that fish only grow to the size that's available. 'So I was confident of this and thought there'll be a term for a creature that only grows to the available space,' she explains. 'But then I looked it up and I found, to my horror, that fish remain stunted if the water quality is *poor*, so they don't have that quality at all.' Many years later, Rowling created a creature that exhibited this quality. 'The Occamy is quite a frightening choranaptyxic but engaging creature,' she says. 'I had to coin this word because I conceived of this creature that could shrink or grow according to the available space.'

'That is my favourite new word,' says Eddie Redmayne. The actor had a long discussion with a dialogue coach about how the word should be pronounced (co-rah-nap-TISS-ick).

FLIGHT CANCELLED

The earliest designs for the Occamy, submitted by concept artist Rob Bliss, included multiple wings. 'There were bits in the script where we thought we'd see her flying out across the city,' Pablo Grillo. 'It would be great to create the silhouette of this creature with all these wings caterpillaring through the sky.' Instead, the Occamy became room-bound, appearing only in the sequence in the department store's attic storeroom. '[The wings] didn't fit the purpose of it being wrapped in a department store because you'd never see them,' says Christian Manz. 'So we applied it to the Thunderbird instead.' The Occamy moved towards being more snake-like, with the feathered head of a bird of prey. 'This was a hard creature to get right,' says Dermot Power. 'She had to look elegant and mysterious but also needed to show a strong maternal side when threatened. To show her in a threatened state, we wanted the Occamy's feathers to have an animated, iridescent quality, so for inspiration we looked to peacocks. We also looked at cuttlefish and chameleons for their changing skin patterns.' The animators also took reference from hummingbirds for the Occamy's feathered head and wings. The plumage on a hummingbird's neck overlap in a manner similar to fish scales, which seems appropriate to the Occamy.

GRAPHIC DESIGN OF ADVERT BY MINA LIMA

THE DISAPPEARING DEMIGUISE

'THE DEMIGUISE HAS THE CAPACITY TO GO FROM BEING VISIBLE TO INVISIBLE, SO THEIR PELTS CAN BE USED TO MAKE INVISIBILITY CLOAKS' – EDDIE REDMAYNE

Newt Scamander rescued a Demiguise named Dougal, but needs to hunt down the creature when it escapes his case. 'This proves a wee bit tricky, because the Demiguise can vanish at will,' Redmayne explains, 'and he also has this capacity to see the future. So he can predict what people are going to do, which makes catching him a bit of a nightmare.'

The fact that fans were finally able to see the creature that provided the material to make an Invisibility Cloak, which was one of the most important artefacts in the Harry Potter story, raised the bar for the creature designers. One inspiration for the animators was a beloved character from *Harry Potter and the Half-Blood Prince*. 'David Yates was very keen to represent the Demiguise like a little old wise man,' says visual effects supervisor Tim Burke. 'And when we tried to get into the character of him, David suggested Jim Broadbent, who'd played Professor Horace Slughorn on the Potter films. We

almost, at one point, discussed shooting some reference with him. We got into the spirit of this little old man who chatted away to himself and imbued that into the Demiguise personality and character.'

Creating a 'look' of invisibility would seem to be a no-brainer: just don't show the creature. But the catch is that the Demiguise transitions between visible and invisible. For their approach, the artists were inspired by the photographic work of Liu Bolin. Bolin is known as 'The Invisible Man,' as he camouflages subjects within the photo's environment, disappearing like a chameleon. 'The lovely thing is that as you move around them,' says Burke, 'with a slight perspective change you will see a difference of relief to it. Suddenly you realize through perspective that there's something there. And we developed that idea for creating the Demiguise's invisibility where he takes up part of the background. It's only when the camera moves that you see the shift in perspective.'

HAIR CARE

The Demiguise looks a bit like a cross between a primate and a sloth, with huge, owl-like eyes. Hair covers its entire body, described as silvery and long. The visual effects team was also challenged to render believable hair not only in close-ups but when the Demiguise was running fast with its hair moving in the wind. To achieve this, the animators used a proprietary hair grooming toolset called Furtility.

CAPTURING THE CREATURES

Dougal the Demiguise and the new-born Occamy are recovered in the storeroom of the department store, built on a Leavesden sound-stage. 'Another thing I love about Jo's writing,' says Eddie Redmayne, 'is not only has she created Newt's relationship with the animals, but also the relationships between animals. The Demiguise loves the Occamys, and is kind of babysitting them. When one of the Occamys escapes, the Demiguise goes out into the real world, which is a wildly terrifying place for Dougal. He goes out there to make sure that the little newborn Occamy is going to be okay.'

CAPTURING HEARTS

'The Demiguise can see different versions of the future, which means he can predict who is most likely to catch him,' says director David Yates. 'Therefore, it is the least likely person who has the best chance of catching a Demiguise.'

✳

DAN FOGLER WORE A WEIGHTED BACKPACK TO GIVE HIM THE FEEL OF THE DEMIGUISE WHILE REHEARSING.

✳

The quartet needs to get the Demiguise and Occamy back into Newt's case, but Eddie Redmayne claims that there's more than that going on at the time. 'He sends Jacob and Queenie off in one direction while he and Tina get closer to the Demiguise.

'In order to surprise him, Newt has to appear entirely relaxed and unpredictable, but the Demiguise knows him; he already has a sense of what he's going to do. So Newt encourages Tina to just be casual. That it's going to be up to her to catch the Demiguise, because he knows less about her.' Redmayne considers this an important moment between Newt and Tina. 'I think that not only is Newt trying to find the Demiguise, but subconsciously he's beginning to enjoy the proximity with Tina,' says the actor.

During the chase after the Demiguise and Occamy, Jacob also has a moment — not with Queenie, but with Dougal. 'Jacob becomes very friendly with the Demiguise' says Dan Fogler. 'For some reason, there's something in Jacob's nature that lets him feel that I'm not a threat. So there are these really sweet moments where the chaos is happening and the Demiguise jumps up into my arms. And I'm like, "It's okay, buddy, it's gonna be okay."'

ONE FOR THE POT

The sequence to capture the Occamy, which has grown enough to fill the space's store-room, was made that much more complicated because it had to be filmed sequentially. 'As the Occamy gets more agitated and does more destruction, we have to actually destroy the set,' Tim Burke explains. 'When it's startled it's not aggressive, but when it's frightened, because it's so big, it's clumsy, and its awkwardness means that it knocks a *lot* of things over.' The store weathers quite a bit of destruction before Newt captures the creature, with the help of Tina, Jacob, and Queenie, and stores it in a teapot.

While rehearsing the scene the actors would often have a puppet to work with before the final takes. 'But they take the puppet out of the shot so you're seeing us imagining these creatures and doing a lot of pantomime to make it seem as if they're there,' says Fogler. 'It's really nice to see Newt interacting with the creatures and Eddie does it brilliantly.'

STAGING A FUNDRAISING BA

WHITE TIE GALA REQUIRED VINTAGE CLOTHES AND VINTAGE VEHICLES

To support his son's re-election campaign for the New York Senate — and the possibility of a run for president of the United States — the *Clarion* newspaper's owner and media mogul, Henry Shaw Senior, holds a fundraising dinner at City Hall. This white-tie affair was attended by the moneyed and the elite of New York City.

The Shaw Banquet was one of the few sequences not shot at Leavesden Studios. After scouting New York City and other environments, production designer Stuart Craig was able to find a suitable location in Liverpool. 'There was kind of a cross influence between Liverpool and New York, because of transatlantic shipping. Liverpool was a prosperous, cosmopolitan port city in the way that New York was,' Craig explains. 'It was thriving and had the kind of money available in America, with the same optimistic confidence to build these beautiful, enormous buildings, very American in spirit and of the period.' Craig chose St. George's Hall, a magnificent public hall built in the Neoclassical style, for City Hall, New York.

NQUET FOR SENATOR SHAW

'I was thrilled to bring *Fantastic Beasts and Where to Find Them* to a city that has such fond memories for me,' says producer David Heyman. 'My mother is from Liverpool and, as a child, we would often visit family there. The architecture in this beautiful city worked perfectly for our film.'

The floor of St George's was raised and then exactly recreated in large tiles that were laid down upon the original. Rows and rows of white tablecloth-covered round tables were set upon that, surrounded by black faux bamboo chairs. Bunting of American flags was hung around the room. 'It looked amazing,' says Josh Cowdery, (Senator Shaw). 'The tables looked great. Everyone dressed nineteen-twenties to the nines. Everyone in the crowd was actually doing a character. All that detail in the room made it easier to feel like giving a real speech,' he adds. 'If it was just a green screen and five guys in front of me, where everything would be added later, that would have been tougher.'

PICTURE PERFECT

Josh Cowdery was aware that there would be a huge portrait of Senator Shaw's face in the room — he had read it in the script. He had no idea, however, how large it would be and how it had been made. 'The first day I saw it, I really just assumed they must have had some great printer. Then, on the second or third day, I looked at it and thought, that's really incredible detail. I noticed it was canvas, and saw what looked like paintbrush strokes, so I went to David [Yates] and asked, did someone paint that? And he started laughing.' Cowdery was stunned. 'Someone had hung it up in a studio, and with a photo in hand had painted my face, like, fifty feet high. It's huge and it's funny; I know my mom would like it.'

Portrait painter Barnaby Gorton, who also painted the hanging portrait of President Picquery in MACUSA, was given references of Cowdery and images from Franklin Delano Roosevelt's campaign posters from the 1940s to follow for style. In fact, 'We needed two paintings of Senator Shaw,' explains Gorton, 'in case the first one was damaged or destroyed in its fall.' When the room is attacked by the manic force that has been tearing up the city, the poster comes loose and lands on Senator Shaw, killing him. 'Just to do one painting that size is impressive,' says Gorton. 'Doing two together, wow.'

SMASHING STUNTS

Senator Henry Shaw's brother, Langdon Shaw (Ronan Rafferty), had earlier brought the Barebone family to the *Clarion* offices, informing his father that they had a huge story to tell about the disturbances in the city being caused by witchcraft. Henry Sr tiredly told them to leave, but Henry Jr did him one worse — he called them freaks, and told Credence to put a dropped flyer in the trash, 'where they all belong.'

At the Shaw dinner, the Obscurus lays waste to the interior of City Hall, sending the gala guests flying like autumn leaves. 'We wanted our stunties to hit the tables hard and come off them with a lot of energy,' says stunt coordinator Eunice

Huthart. 'It was not something that they could run and jump themselves.' A large amount of stunt men and women were attached to wires that would pull them up and back. Huthart called the scene 'a stunt team's dream. We got people flying up, crashing on tables, crashing down.' The chairs and tables were of breakaway foam, of course. 'It was pretty gnarly,' Huthart says. 'We did it in three takes. I had a little bet with my wire guy, who said it would take three. I said four. I would have liked to have gone four,' she says with a smile. 'I just like to smash things up.'

GRAVES DETAINS POSSIBLE SUSPECTS

A MACUSA EMPLOYEE AND FOREIGN VISITOR ARE TAKEN INTO CUSTODY AS POSSIBLE SUSPECTS INVOLVED IN CAUSING THE MAGICAL FORCE THAT IS THREATENING TO EXPOSE WIZARDKIND TO THE NO-MAJS.

After the Erumpent is recovered, Tina brings Newt's case (with Newt and Jacob within) to show MACUSA's president — and inadvertently winds up showing it to the entire International Confederation of Wizards, who are discussing what could have magically murdered Senator Shaw. Tina explains that there are magical creatures inside the case, some of which had escaped, and after Newt and Jacob emerge, it's immediately assumed one of Newt's beasts is the killer. But Newt knows better. Seeing the marks on a magical projection of Shaw's body that floats above the assembly, Newt declares that he was killed by an Obscurus. Picquery denies that there could be an Obscurial in America, and orders Graves to impound the case and arrest Newt and Tina. Jacob is also incarcerated, presumably to be Obliviated.

INTERROGATION MAY PROVIDE ANSWERS TO MYSTERIOUS FORCE RAZING CITY

Newt and Tina are brought to a square, metal-walled investigation room where Graves goes over Newt's background, especially curious about Newt being expelled from Hogwarts for endangering human life with a beast. He wonders why one of his professors, Albus Dumbledore, would argue against his expulsion. What makes Dumbledore so fond of him? He also suggests that Newt released the creatures deliberately, to expose wizardkind and provoke a war. Newt understands his thinly veiled accusation — that this could have caused a mass slaughter for the greater good. But Newt claims that he is not a follower of Grindelwald, who strives for a war between wizards and non-magical folk 'for the greater good.'

To Newt's horror, Graves has removed the Obscurus from Newt's case, and is fascinated by it. To reassure Tina, Newt explains that it could not hurt anyone in its current form. When Graves asks for confirmation that the Obscurus is useless without its host, Newt asks back, 'What on earth would you use it for'?

The interrogation ends with Graves accusing Newt of trying to break the Statute of Secrecy and sentencing him and Tina to death.

GRAPHIC DESIGN OF ADVERT BY MINA LIMA

MOMENTS OF GLORY

Pickett the Bowtruckle is given a chance to show off his braver side when he picks the locks on Newt's handcuffs and releases him to disarm the executioners. Newt unleashes the Swooping Evil as well. Unfortunately, when one of the executioner's wands lands in the pool's potion, it causes Tina's memories to become dark and sorrowful, but mercifully relieves her of her dazed state. By using the back of the Swooping Evil as it flies by, Tina is able to jump to safety in Newt's arms.

At the same time, Queenie's Legilimens powers have alerted her to her sister and friends' dilemma. She manages to take Jacob into her custody, recover Newt's case, and leave MACUSA with Tina, Jacob, and Newt inside it after using her charms on a flustered Abernathy.

INSIDE THE DEATH CELL

Newt and Tina are handcuffed and escorted by two executioners to the Death Cell, which houses only a chair suspended magically over a square pool of a dark liquid.

'The death chamber, I suppose, was very unexpected,' says Stuart Craig. 'It's down in the bowels of this place, below the basement levels, in the foundation. The ceiling is created by massive cast iron beams, which are the very foundation of the building. These give the sense that you are deep, deep, deep underground, which helps the secret, sinister connotations of the place.'

Craig and director David Yates wanted to give the room a clinical feel. The walls resemble white marble, 'like a mortuary,' says Craig, 'or for post-mortems, basically. It's an exercise in architectural brutality.' VFX supervisor Christian Manz has his own impressions of the room and its use. 'It's hard to say it's not beautiful, but the death cell scene to me was cold and weird, and probably a shock to the audience. It's very stark and so eerie — everybody's eerily nice but they're putting you to death.'

As the procedure begins, an executioner uses her wand to extract pleasant memories from the accused and places them into the liquid. 'The initial design was inspired by an installation at the Saatchi Gallery [in London] in which there was oil with a perfect reflection on the surface,' says Manz, who created the pool digitally. 'Using the language people remember from the Potter films of the Pensieve, the idea is that there are tendrils floating on this beautiful surface and you see the memories get cast in.'

The good memories are used to subdue the prisoner, calming them and making the idea of stepping into the chair inviting. As Tina floats above the pool, we see images from her childhood with Queenie before their parents died. Another happy memory of Tina's reveals why she was demoted from her job as an Auror — saving Credence from being beaten by Mary Lou.

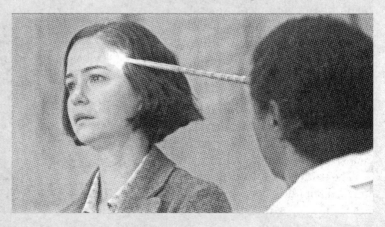

NSPS MEMBERS FOUND MURDERED

That same day, Mary Lou Barebone, leader of the New Salem Philanthropic Society, is found dead within the Second Salem Church. Her body bears scars similar to those seen on the body of Senator Henry Shaw Jr after he was killed earlier by an Obscurus during a fundraising banquet held at City Hall.

Percival Graves, Director of Magical Security for MACUSA, was in the vicinity of the crime scene, and discovers not only the body of Mary Lou Barebone but also her eldest adopted daughter, Chastity, within the destroyed building. The whereabouts of Barebone's two other adopted children — son, Credence, and younger daughter, Modesty — are unknown.

DEFINING THE OBSCURUS

MACUSA President Madam Seraphina Picquery announces that the Dark Force causing destruction in the city and threatening the possibility of exposure with the No-Maj world has been eradicated. The entity was discovered to be an Obscurus.

'You know, some of the fantastic beasts get out of Newt's case and our characters have to track them down and bring them back,' says director David Yates, 'but the real story is about a beast that exists within, the beast that is unknowable until we get to the final act of the movie. That's where the real story lies, I think.'

'The truth is that Credence is magical, and he's been repressing his magic,' says Ezra Miller.

MYSTERIOUS DARK FORCE DISCOVERED

'The forces of the universe come into a physical form, which is an Obscurus, and that Obscurus initially comes to an Obscurial as a friend, encouraging them, then with increasing severity to

encourage this kid to allow their true identity and true power to run through them. The idea of this Obscurus is that if you continue to repress the truth of *you*, it turns ugly. It becomes something actually destructive, and then it comes to this place where you can no longer run from who you are, and you can't run from the things you're afraid of.

'It's something I know,' Miller continues. 'That's something, I think, a lot of people know from experience in their own lives, is that these things catch up to you eventually. And if you repress it, then it's probably just going to mean that when it does catch up to you, there are gonna be heavier consequences, and it's gonna be a harder reality to deal with.'

FORMING THE OBSCURUS

'**W**hether the Obscurus is a creature or not is a difficult question,' says Pablo Grillo. 'It's the embodiment of the twisted and repressed magic of Credence. It's described as a black mass, a dark force. An ambiguous shape-shifting form, which could be any size, but had to ultimately express his inner rage, his fury, his confusion. To be able to express those things through such an ambiguous mass is a great challenge.'

'[The Obscurus] was a bit of a journey,' admits Tim Burke. 'We didn't really know what it was. It was unlike all the other creatures where we could draw things and then interpret them into models and start animating them. This thing had no form. It was rage, it was anger. So we went through the usual thing of trying to find reference of what it might move like, but it was really Ezra's character that was going to drive the Obscurus itself.'

And Ezra Miller played a big role in how the final version of Obscurus came to look. 'I asked Ezra to let us take some photographs as reference points,' explains Burke. 'We were on an empty stage and had my camera with me, and Ezra asked, would you mind if I give you my impression of what it would be like? We were just going to shoot some still photos, but instead videotaped it. He gave an amazing, terrifying performance, screaming and thrashing about. It was anger and rage in a physical form,

> **'THIS THING HAD NO FORM. IT WAS RAGE. IT WAS ANGER,'**
> **– TIM BURKE**

with this incredible guttural noise,' he remembers. Miller was exhausted after just three minutes.

'We edited it and played it at different speeds, and reversed it. David Yates wasn't even aware that Ezra had done this stuff,' Burke continues. 'When we showed it to him, David was blown away by it, he just said, "Wow, this is our Obscurus." Ezra really helped us by his movements and his vocalization. His performance gave the Obscurus a real character, even though it was an abstract thing.'

Then Miller's performance was turned into an animated form. 'The Obscurus was just a constantly changing, membranous sort of quality and then the particles came along afterward,' said Burke. Bespoke tools were created for the Obscurus, as it needed to move differently in different places, such as Times Square, the subway, or in the air.

REVEALING EMOTIONS

Another aspect of the Obscurus's look and movements was that it needed to convey emotion, 'so when it's angry, it has a fiery inside while it's lashing out and throwing things,' Tim Burke explains. 'Then, when Tina talks to it, it calms down as if it's listening and becomes this beautiful sculpture-like piece of art. It's quite beautiful, swirling and mesmerizing — it's definitely not your usual movie visual effects.'

If the visual effects crew wanted this featureless object to convey emotion, they succeeded. 'One audience member from an early screening told me they never thought they would have feelings for a black blob.'

AURORS BATTLE IN CITY HALL SUBWAY

Pursued by Newt Scamander, who races over the rooftops trying to head off Aurors that are trying to kill it, the Obscurus winds its way through the city streets leaving shop fronts shattered and cars upturned and smashed. After a confrontation with the New York City Police, the Obscurus slams into the ground just outside of the City Hall subway station entrance.

The original City Hall Station in New York was built in 1904, and was notable not only for leaded skylights and stylish chandeliers but for not having any straight lines. The architecture inside reflects this, with vaulted ceilings and curved entryways. Being the last station on its line, the train would make a U-turn at City Hall to go back uptown.

'That City Hall station still exists, but you're not allowed to go there,' says Stuart Craig. 'We applied for permission to just take photographs and were not allowed. I imagine there's some safety reason, and that's a perfectly good explanation.

'Research is so much easier these days: do an online search,' Craig continues. 'It's just transformed what we do totally, so it was really pretty easy to research.' Craig and the designers turned to photographs, archived records, and even novels for descriptions of the station. 'We were fairly faithful [in] the production of City Hall. The style is early Art Deco, but it has a real credibility because it is impermeable, which subways are, being damp, underground spaces. We retained the name and created a big, open concourse with a subway leading into it that gets smashed up in the final showdown,' with, as Craig puts it, 'carnage and wreckage everywhere.'

The full Investigative Team and the other Aurors from MACUSA enter the station and fight the destructive magical force that has been demolishing parts of lower Manhattan against not only Newt and Tina's appeals, but Graves's as well. At battle's end, they believe they have eliminated it.

AN ATTENTION TO DETAIL

The City Hall Subway set includes a plaque resembling those hung in the real New York subways, which give attribution to the craftsmen that funded, managed, or constructed it. This City Hall's plaque lists names from the art department.

DIRECTOR OF MAGICAL SECURITY USED FOR DISGUISE

GRINDELWALD CAPTURED!

WHERE IS PERCIVAL GRAVES?

Subsequent to the Obscurus's destruction, Percival Graves, Head of the Department of Magical Law Enforcement, is uncovered by a Revelio spell to be Gellert Grindelwald.

After the Obscurus is destroyed, Graves is seething and begins spouting anti-Statute rhetoric, questioning who this law protects. 'A law that has us scuttling like rats in a gutter. A law that demands that we conceal our true nature. A law that directs those under its dominion to cower in fear lest we risk discovery.' Graves states that he would refuse to bow down any longer.

Though President Picquery asks the Aurors to relieve Graves of his wand, he does not do so, and begins firing spells at them. Graves appears to be winning, but suddenly Newt Scamander, who was initially suspected

of causing the destruction, releases one of his creatures: the Swooping Evil. It shields the Aurors enough that Scamander is able to wrap a rope of light around him and keep him immobile until Tina Goldstein is able to get Graves's wand. It is then Scamander utters the Revelio spell, and Graves transforms into Grindelwald.

REFRESHING RAIN SOAKS CITY
THUNDERBIRD AN OPPORTUNITY TO OBLIVIATE NO-MAJ POPULATION

Though Gellert Grindelwald was revealed and captured, Madam Picquery still needed to handle the exposure the No-Majs had to the extensive amount of magical activity caused by the Obscurus, and especially to the last battle that took down Grindelwald. It was not possible, in her eyes, to Obliviate the entire city, but was helped by Scamander.

FRANK BEGINNINGS

'The Thunderbird was the real reason Newt is in New York,' says Eddie Redmayne. 'He says he's there to get an Appaloosa Puffskein as a gift for a friend, but that's just the excuse he's using to be there.' (It does not seem to faze him when Tina tells him that the buying and selling of magical beasts in New York is strictly forbidden.) 'Thunderbirds are incredibly valuable and this bird had been trafficked to Egypt, where Newt finds him,' Redmayne continues. 'So he brings him back to the States in order to release him in his native Arizona. He wants to put Frank back where he belongs.'

TAKING FLIGHT

The animators had originally designed the Occamy with the idea of multiple wings, an idea that changed when the story restricted the beast to scenes within the storeroom. 'So we moved the Occamy more toward a dragon and decided to use the multiple wings with the Thunderbird,' says Pablo Grillo.

Then, 'the Thunderbird being the bookend of the film where Newt's real purpose is to release it back into the world, it felt important that it has a certain poise and nobility to it,' he explains. 'Inspiration came from the bald eagle, the dignity and nobility of birds of prey. Incredible, statuesque, and with its multiple wings, a beautiful way of flying.'

One challenge to the visual development artists was to conceive how the creature's four pairs of wings could all fold together against his body. 'Then we wanted to add something else to make it more fantastical,' says Dermot Power. 'The idea came from the name of the creature.' Power created artwork that depicted its thunderous state, 'reflecting stormy clouds, darkening the feathers as it releases its energy.'

'The blood-flow across his feathers creates the impression of cloud-like patterns moving through him,' says

CONTINUED ON PAGE 79

FIRST AND LAST IMPRESSIONS

When Newt Scamander took Jacob inside his case to show him his beasts, Frank was the first one he greeted. 'And, again, such a brilliant idea from Jo [Rowling],' says Redmayne: 'The Thunderbird has this extraordinary quality that he can sense danger, and his mood is reflected by the weather that pours from beneath from him. So if he's frightened or excited then the rain pours.'

'Frank was a lovely creature to bookend the film,' says Pablo Grillo. 'He plays a fundamental role: he goes up and sends out a potion that's going to make all of New York forget what they've just seen. It wraps the film up beautifully because in the end, the whole purpose of Newt going to America was to deal with this beast, to release it back into the wild, and it was an incredible thing to show [that]. I think it's a great symbol, in that sense of hope that it will do well.'

RAINY DAY MAGIC

Frank is excited by Newt's return, expressed by a sudden shower. This led a new wizarding convention contributed by the actor. 'I got this idea that I could use my wand as an umbrella,' he says. When Redmayne suggested this to director David Yates, he was told 'I love it, use it.' The concept that a wand can shield a wizard from the elements is used again at the end of the film by Queenie when she steps out onto the street to say a touching and regretful goodbye to Jacob Kowalski before he walks into the rain — but not before she suggests they should go somewhere and be together.

CONTINUED ON FROM 78

Christian Manz. 'And when he is creating sunlight, his wings act almost like a stained-glass window with the light coming through them. Rain does not come from him directly, but as he is flying and beating his wings, he is drawing water vapour in and around him to create clouds and, therefore, rain.'

LATE REVIEW:

KOWALSKI'S BAKERY

A new business opens up on the Lower East Side of New York: Kowalski's Bakery, owned by No-Maj Jacob Kowalski. The building front is reminiscent of the many immigrant-owned businesses started in the early 1900s, particularly the Vesuvio Bakery, which displayed its bread and pastries in two wide storefront windows under a scalloped awning.

As with all the other No-Majs in New York, owner Jacob Kowalski's memory of the Obscurus attack and damage was wiped out by standing in the rain that carried the Swooping Evil venom extract. Seemingly stuck back at the canning factory, his luck is changed by a gift Newt Scamander leaves for him: silver Occamy shells that will act as collateral for a bank loan. These allow Jacob to finally get his bakery. 'But there's this subliminal sort of memory that's coming out in the cakes and the bread he's making,' says prop modeller Pierre Bohanna. Pastry versions of Demiguises, Nifflers, Erumpents, and Occamys are sold alongside the rolls and paczki. 'We had this wonderfully fun prop-making job of producing pastries and breads in the shapes of the creatures,' Bohanna remembers. 'But obviously they're not *real* breads.' The set designers and prop makers had learned their lesson providing food for the Great Hall feasts in the Harry Potter films: baked goods and hot lights do not make an edible combination. 'These are synthetics, cast in moulds. But they're artworks, in a beautiful way, with convincing finishes and feel. That's what prop making is all about,' Bohanna continues, 'doing something like that and making it work, making it believable.'

The shop runs a bustling business, and the store is crowded when a flash of pink enters and Jacob greets his latest customer. It's Queenie, beaming, radiant. Jacob touches his neck and then smiles.

EXTRA! EXTRA! EXTRA! EXTRA! EXTRA! EXTRA! EXTRA! EXTRA!

A BEHIND-THE-SCENES PREVIEW OF

FANTASTIC BEASTS

THE CRIMES OF GRINDELWALD™

GELLERT GRINDELWALD ESCAPES!

D ark wizard Gellert Grindelwald manages to escape the guards assigned to him by the Magical Congress of the United States of America while being extradited to Europe to serve time for his crimes.

'Grindelwald is such a villain and he so enjoys it,' says Alison Sudol. 'There's something very fun about being bad and having a really good time with it.' Sudol also notes that Grindelwald, played by Johnny Depp, is quite the chameleon. 'Grindelwald's one way to one person and then another way to another person,' she explains, 'and it's obviously an incredibly destructive, terrible characteristic to have as a human but quite fun to play as an actor.'

CREDENCE BAREBONE

DISCOVERED ALIVE AND IN EUROPE

Credence, the missing adopted son of the late Mary Lou Barebone, is spotted at Circus Arcanus, which recently completed a run in New York and is now touring Europe.

'[Credence] has cast off the chains of his abuse and repression,' says actor Ezra Miller. 'He has an awareness of his relationship with the Obscurus, and is gaining control to manifest it intentionally. He is setting out on a journey of self-discovery,' Miller continues, 'because much of what he knew of himself he knows now to be a lie.'

SCAMANDER'S FANTASTIC BEASTS AND WHERE TO FIND THEM BOOK PUBLISHED!

Flourish & Blotts proudly announces a launch and signing for the publication by Obscurus Books of the first book from Magizoologist Newt Scamander, *Fantastic Beasts and Where to Find Them*. This occasion showcases the author's quest to educate the wizarding world about these extraordinary creatures.

'Newt's book has been published and it's made him a bit of a celebrity,' says Eddie Redmayne, 'which he finds brilliantly awkward.

Newt's a unique fellow; his interest in creatures and beasts is unique to him, and he remains true to his passion.' Redmayne feels that Newt is more of a lone wolf than he'd like to admit and 'doesn't want to be pulled to anyone's side. Yet because the stakes going on in the world are so high now, he's being pulled in different directions. Part of his journey now is Newt realizing that although he has his own passions, and that he's always taken his own route through life, there come moments when you have to choose a side.'

NEWT SCAMANDER

FANTASTIC BEASTS

AND WHERE TO FIND THEM

OBSCURUS

PORPENTINA GOLDSTEIN
Reappointed as Auror at MACUSA

As a result of her role in the capture of Gellert Grindelwald, Tina Goldstein is reinstated as an Auror for MACUSA. 'At the beginning of the second film, Tina's been an Auror for a while now, and is thriving in that position,' says Katherine Waterston. But Waterston believes her character learned some important lessons when she was relegated to the Wand Permit Office. 'Although she was nervous about her career, she never fully lost her confidence in following her instincts,' she explains. 'Her following those instincts led to Grindelwald's arrest! When you see her now, she's back in the thick of it.'

TRAVEL
RECOMMENDATION:
PARIS 1927

Fantastic Beasts: The Crimes of Grindelwald visits familiar locations in New York and London before travelling to a new one: Paris. 'Paris at this time was just such an extraordinary part of the world,' says Eddie Redmayne. 'It was where a melting pot of people were meeting, and new paths were being forged. This was really a time of change, a change in fashion, a change in architecture. Art Deco was moving into Art Nouveau. It was an incredibly colourful and vibrant place.' During his time there, Newt Scamander will visit many magical locations, all of which will be making their debut in the Wizarding World.

GRINDELWALD SEARCH RECEIVES HELP FROM A YOUNG OLD FRIEND

Aurors from the Ministry of Magic pay a visit to Hogwarts, where Albus Dumbledore is currently one of the teaching staff.

Dumbledore is played by actor Jude Law, who couldn't resist rewatching the performances of Michael Gambon and Richard Harris for his own interpretation. 'First of all, it was an obvious opportunity to watch all the films again, which was really fun,' he says, 'and I just wanted to see if there was anything I could eke from them, even though it was very important to all of us that we weren't creating that Dumbledore. We were creating a man who was going to become that Dumbledore.'

CUPID'S CORNER:
QUEENIE GOLDSTEIN AND JACOB KOWALSKI

Regardless of her affection for the now-successful No-Maj baker, Jacob Kowalski, Queenie Goldstein is still aware of the prohibition on relationships between magical and non-magical people. 'At the end of the first film, she's breaking the rules by coming back to Jacob,' says Alison Sudol. 'Because she's been seeing into people's heads for so long, she's never fallen in love the way that she falls in love with Jacob, and I think she's a bit desperate to not to lose that. It pushes her to make perhaps not the wisest of choices, which we've all done in love.' Dan Fogler admits that it's tough to think about a relationship when the wizarding world is in such a tenuous state. 'The dial on the boiler is clicking toward hotter,' he says. 'The stakes are rising and everyone's picking sides, which makes the relationships more serious, and more complex.'

LUMOS ON THE MINISTRY OF MAGIC:

THESEUS SCAMANDER AND LETA LESTRANGE

Theseus Scamander is Head of the Ministry of Magic's Auror Department, involved in the pursuit of Gellert Grindelwald, and Newt Scamander's older brother. 'Theseus is the polar opposite of Newt,' says actor Callum Turner. 'He's high up in the Ministry, and that's how he fights the good fight. Newt and he are on the same side, just fighting in a different way.

But no matter what, they're brothers and they love each other.'

Leta Lestrange also works for the Ministry. 'I knew there was history between her and Newt,' says actress Zoë Kravitz, though Leta is now engaged to his brother. 'Leta comes from a pureblood wizarding family. And because of that, Leta's quite complicated,' she says with a smile.

CONNECT-THE-PLOTS

What I love about this new film is the connective tissue' says Eddie Redmayne. 'That those names, the stories, the histories that sit in the back of our minds from the Potter series begin to weave their way into Beasts, whether it's through Leta Lestrange or Dumbledore's arrival, to the Elder Wand and the return to Hogwarts, which I just loved. You'll see the role of the first Fantastic Beasts film, set within just a couple of days, was actually a moment within a much bigger history.'

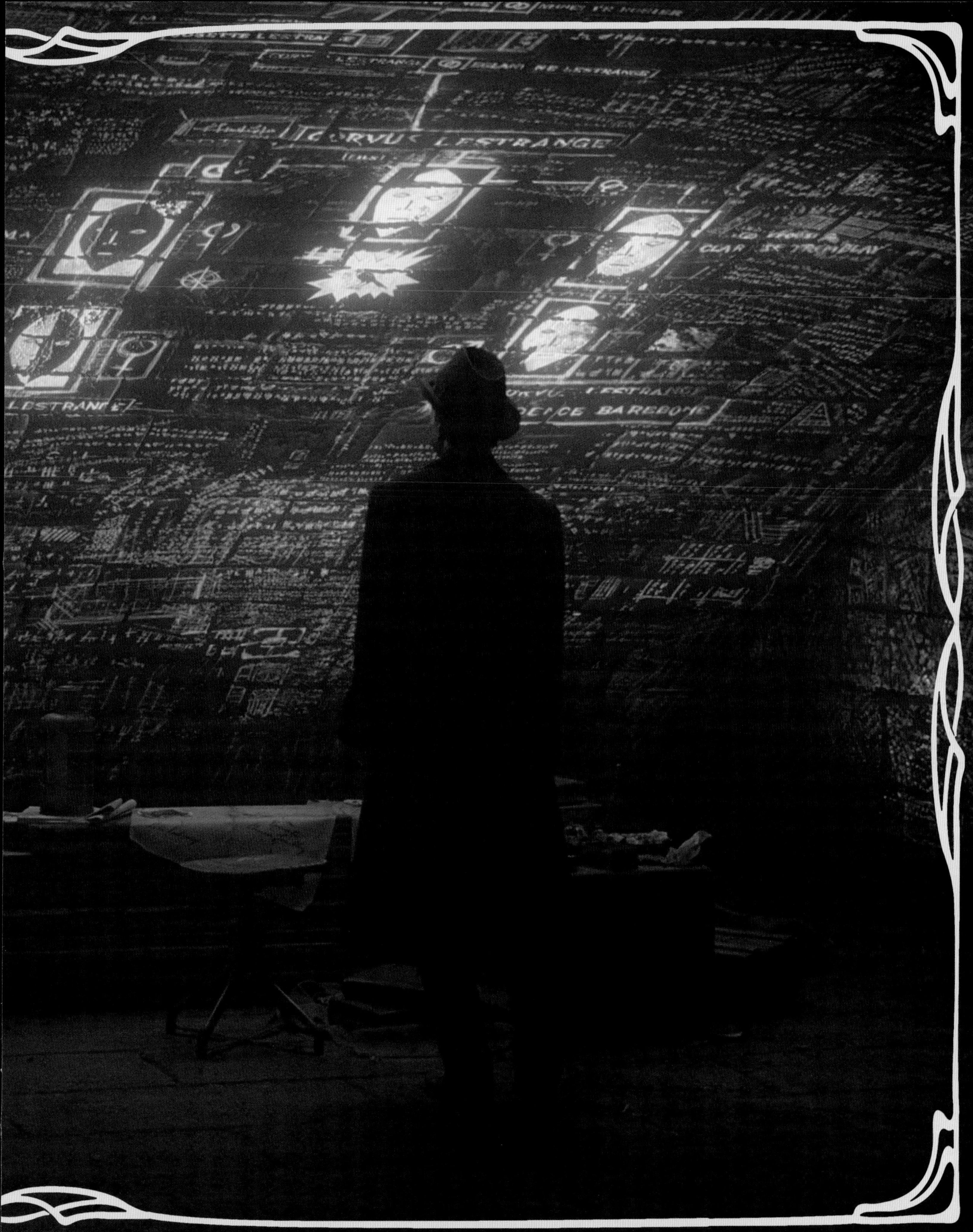
LESTRANGE

FAMILIAR FANTASTIC BEASTS RETURN; NEW BEASTS MAKE THEIR DEBUT

Pickett the Bowtruckle and the Niffler will return to the big screen in *Fantastic Beasts: The Crimes of Grindelwald*. A visit to the London home of Newt Scamander will premiere new beasts, and Circus Arcanus also showcases new creatures, including an enormous, formidable beast.